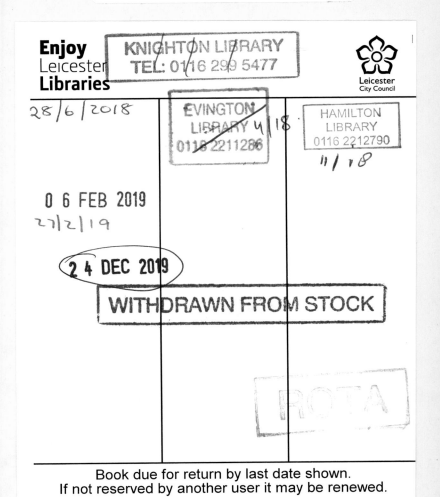

Enjoy Leicester **Libraries**

Book due for return by last date shown.
If not reserved by another user it may be renewed.

24/7 – Renewals, Reservations, Catalogue

www.leicester.gov.uk/libraries

Charges may be payable on overdue items

ERNEST H. SHEPARD

Drawn from Life

METHUEN

Published by Methuen 2002

1 3 5 7 9 10 8 6 4 2

First published in 1961
© 1961 Ernest Shepard

This paperback edition published by Methuen Publishing Ltd
215 Vauxhall Bridge Rd, London SW1V 1EJ

Methuen Publishing Limited Reg. No. 3543167

A CIP catalogue record for this book is available from the British Library

ISBN 0 413 77248 9

Printed and bound in Great Britain
by Creative Print and Design Ltd (Wales), Ebbw Vale

TO
MY DAUGHTER MARY

Pie and I soon after we became engaged.
Taken at Norbury 1904

CONTENTS

PREFACE

I WROTE *Drawn from Memory* because I had always promised my children that I would one day write down the memories of my childhood which I had been in the habit of telling them verbally. The writing, and the drawing of the accompanying illustrations, afforded me much private pleasure; but when the result was published I did not expect to receive encouragement to embark upon the description of a further stage of my life. But encouragement was what I received in good measure; and, fortified thus by the good wishes of friends and the blessing of my publisher, I have tried my hand again.

The first book covered roughly a year of my boyhood. It was an important year outside the Shepard family circle – 1887, the year of Queen Victoria's Golden Jubilee. Within my family it was a period of peace before a storm. We were living in our house by Regent's Park, and I see myself riding my tricycle horse up and down the terrace pavement in untroubled bliss.

The second book begins with the illness and death of my mother in 1890, when I was ten years old, a bereavement which entirely altered our family life. It covers the period of my adolescence and early manhood up to my marriage in 1904. Some of the friendships I made in those years have endured to the present day, and, to my surprise, I have found that some of the letters I wrote then have survived. I am particularly grateful to Chattie Salaman for lending me some letters which include drawings that I have reproduced. I am also indebted to Alan White for his help and advice in arranging my book, and above all I am deeply grateful to Norah for her unfailing help and encouragement.

PREFACE

It may surprise some of my readers to hear that when I married, my wife and I were able to live perfectly comfortably on twenty-one shillings a week, of which only 2s. 3½d. went on the rent of our cottage in Surrey. But such facts, which contrast so sharply with conditions at the present time, seem to me some justification in themselves for presenting this account of one kind of life at the turn of the century.

E. H. S.

Chapter One

LIFE WITH THE AUNTS

IN the middle of April 1890 we three children – my sister Ethel, my brother Cyril and myself – were sent away from our home in Kent Terrace. We did not know why; still less did we guess that we were never to go back. My mother, lying in bed, said good-bye quite cheerfully, as though we were leaving for a short visit, and we detected nothing in her appearance to tell us that we should not see her again. She had been ill for over a year and it had become part of our daily life to carry her meals upstairs to her bedroom and to push her wheel-chair on our walks round the park. We would sit round her bed in the evening and tell her of our day's adventures, and Ethel would sometimes write a letter for her. We did not know that her illness had recently taken a turn for the worse and that Father had been warned that she had not long to live. The decision to send us away must have been a hard one for him to take, but it was a wise one, for it spared both Mother and us the sorrow of parting. He knew we should be well cared for at our Aunts' and that we should not be far away.

We had a warm welcome at the house in Gordon Square. Even Aunt Annie, the invalid, brightened up and invited us to sit on her couch while we prattled away. The house was just the same as it had been three years before when we had stayed there for a fortnight in the Easter holidays. The imposing hat-stand in the hall was adorned with more of Father's cast-off hats; the Albatross head hanging on the wall was perhaps a trifle more moth-eaten; the hand-bell, brightly polished and ready to announce the advent of a meal, was still on its stand; and last but by no means least, there was the ever-present smell of dinner. One addition to the dining-room was a 'Fernery' of solid iron construction with a domed top reminiscent

of the Crystal Palace. It was not unlike a tea-trolley on wheels surmounted by a glass conservatory filled with ferns. The ferns were diligently tended by Aunt Fanny and Aunt Emily, who had collected them on their visits to the country. Aunt Emily's plants never seemed to thrive; I suspect they received too inquisitive attention from her, for she was constantly disturbing them to see if they were 'making root'. Moreover, there were frequent disagreements between the Aunts as to the wisdom of opening or shutting a ventilator in the roof. The glass top of the fernery was always steamed over, so that it was not easy to see what botanical developments were taking place inside.

Of my two other aunts the eldest, Alicia, spent most of her time in an unequal battle with the weekly accounts, while Aunt Annie, a trifle paler and more wan, lay on her couch all day.

The maids, five in number, were the same as before – Edlin the cook, Jane the parlourmaid, Alice and Mary the housemaids, and the little one at the end whose name I could never remember and whom I had no means of identifying. The erstwhile charwoman had left under a cloud with a few pounds of butter smuggled in her basket, and Henry the odd man was odder than ever. The maids trooped into morning prayers at ten o'clock; evening prayers were at nine in the drawing-room, and I was now deemed old enough to attend the ceremony and afterward to carry my candle upstairs to my bedroom on the top floor, a long journey in semi-darkness. There I was condemned to sleep alone, for Cyril had been given a small room on the floor below.

Soon after our arrival we were told that Mother was worse. We were troubled, but even so did not realize the seriousness of her condition. I never dreamed that she *could* die. A few days later Aunt Alicia called us together in her study and told us that Mother had died early that morning. It must have been an ordeal for my aunts to have three heart-broken and bewildered children in their care, and their kindness was beyond words. In three days Father joined us, and it was a consolation to us to have him, as I am sure it was also for him to be with us.

When the pain of our grief lessened, Cyril and I would spend

hours talking over what was ahead of us. We solemnly agreed that we would cry no more, as we knew Mother would not have liked it. And we would not complain about the black clothes and ties we were required to wear. I found an Eton collar particularly irksome after the freedom of my open-necked sailor tunics. We were glad when the blinds were raised and the sunlight streamed in on our darkened lives.

The shock of Mother's death went much deeper than I realized at the time. By temperament I was a resiliently happy child, but this event left a scar for years. I was my mother's youngest child and circumstances drew us very close together. While Cyril and Ethel were at school, I would 'help' her about the house, which of course generally meant getting in her way. She would take me shopping with her and sometimes she would tell me her worries. I enjoyed the outings. We always had fun, and the expeditions frequently ended in the sharing of an ice-cream at Elphinstone's. Elphinstone's sixpenny strawberry ice was so generous as to be almost too large for one small boy, and Mother would take a spoon and raid mine. Our laughter and scrambles were not, however, considered proper by some of the elderly customers; to behave like a schoolgirl was not thought decorous even in a mother as young as she.

I had, I am afraid, a hot temper and often distressed Mother by my outbursts. Afterwards I would creep downstairs, ashamed, to sit beside her, and she would hold my hand and bathe my forehead with eau-de-Cologne and dab my eyes. Then I would sit quietly and listen while she told me about her life as a girl and of the actors and singers who were often at the house in Torrington Square. Her father, William Lee, the water-colour painter, had died when she was a child. He had known a number of artists, and these visited my grandmother (she was only seventeen years older than Mother), so that the house had a Bohemian air. I loved hearing all this, for it was such a contrast to the conventional atmosphere of my father's home.

Mother always encouraged my drawing and, though she had little talent herself, would show me how to use my paints. We made plans together for when I grew up and became an artist myself. She, almost more than Father, inspired me to persevere. After her death I missed her companionship terribly and determined to justify her faith in my talent. So I was particularly glad when Father told me he had taken a studio and that I should be able to practise in it.

He was an architect and adviser to University College Hospital, and for convenience he rented the studio in Gower Street. It was on the first floor, over an artists' colourman's shop, where the students from the Slade School came to buy their paints. I made a habit of going there to do my lessons. Carrying my drawing-book, I would spend hours at work there. Father had a plaster cast of the Venus of Milo: the sketches I made of this cast from every angle were my first attempts at drawing from the antique.

Cyril and I had left the elementary school in Baker Street six months previously, and he had gone as a day boy to St John's Wood Preparatory School in Acacia Road. I was to join him later. I was not looking forward to it, for Cyril's description of life there was, to say the least of it, harrowing. I was glad when Father decided that I should have lessons in his studio until after the summer holidays.

Ethel was able to continue her music at Gordon Square. There was a piano in the back drawing-room, a large room with three windows and a stone balcony overlooking Tavistock Place. She

could practise on the piano while I scraped away on my fiddle. Ethel and I started violin lessons with a Herr Kartenhausen in St John's Wood. He was tall and very fat with a beard so thick that he had difficulty in stowing it away when he played his violin. He had a large family; I never knew just how many children he had, for every time we visited his house a few fresh ones would appear. Frau Kartenhausen spent her time nursing babies. On the whole it was a jolly household, though rather noisy, and music lessons were constantly interrupted. That, however, did not matter, for the 'Herr Doktor', as he called himself, did not teach us much and we soon left. Ethel and I had tea with them one afternoon; for me the meal was spoilt by the detestable presence of caraway seeds in all the cakes and even in the bread. The eldest daughter, a complete *Hausfrau* in miniature, kept order at the table, admonishing the younger children with 'Attention! Now, Elsa and Walther, do not wr-r-r-angle!' while the Herr Doktor drank coffee from a cup fitted with a device to prevent his moustache from getting wet. I had been promoted to a full-sized violin by this time. The instrument was a gift from my godfather and the fingering was far from easy for my small hands. I had to continue my lessons the following autumn at the London Academy of Music in Mortimer Street.

We lived with the Aunts for almost a year. They did all in their power to console us for our loss and make us happy, but though we had the morning-room for our own use, life was not the same as it had been at home. For one thing, we had to tidy up every night and put things away in a cupboard. And then for me there was the bitterness of having to part with Septimus, my beloved tricycle-horse. It was true that he had lost his tail, and in any case I had grown too big for him, but it was nevertheless an agony to see him packed off to a children's hospital. Ethel endured the corresponding sadness of seeing her doll's-house and all its inhabitants dispatched to the same destination. It seemed that all that was left to us were our toy soldiers, but our attempts to parade them on the morning-room floor were not a success, for on the thick carpet they would not stand upright.

As the summer drew near plans were made for the holidays, which we were to spend with our aunts. As neither my godmother, Aunt Alicia, nor Aunt Annie, the invalid, could bear travelling by train, it was their practice to rent a house in the country within easy driving distance of London. This year they chose Wimbledon, then quite a rural place. I remembered my father's description of the Aunts' journey to Highgate three years before, when the 'bus came to a stop on Highgate Hill; and I had hopes of some like adventure on this occasion. The drive, however, was uneventful.

When the 'bus came to Gordon Square to fetch the party, boxes of stores and baskets of linen were stowed on top, Aunts and cages of canaries were packed inside, while Cyril and I were allowed to ride on the box. With the horses trotting in front, this was as good as being on the Atlas 'bus. We crossed Putney Bridge and ascended the hill to a common beyond. This had a windmill standing alone and the driver told us it was Wimbledon Common. The house we were going to was down a side-road off the Ridgeway. It looked fairly new, with large casement windows and virginia creeper on the walls.

Some of the maids must have arrived before we did, for in the drawing-room, which had a grand piano and was crowded with furniture, afternoon tea was already laid. The garden was disappointing – full of shrubs and with no tennis court.

We had not been many days in Wimbledon when, about six o'clock one evening, we heard shouting at the top of our road. Cyril and I rushed out to investigate and found that a haystack on the common was on fire. We joined a small crowd that had gathered to watch, dodging the hot sparks and white smoke that drifted across the road. Someone said that the local volunteer fire brigade had been called. It was a long time in coming, but eventually the engine arrived, pulled by two ill-assorted horses, with the firemen in their

workaday clothes and only brass helmets to identify them. Having witnessed Whiteley's great fire three years before, I was inclined to be critical of their appearance and performance. The manual engine was prepared and pump-handles unstrapped. Then a search for water was made. A pond near by provided it, and volunteers were called for to man the pumps. I tried to join them, but was told that my arms were too short, so I had to stand by and watch. Encouraged by the bystanders, the pumpers got to work. 'Up! Down! Up! Down!' A jet of water shot from the nozzle. Meanwhile some firemen were pulling the rick to pieces with pitchforks. We could not wait to see the end of it all, for Father appeared to call us in to high tea, which we were accustomed to take at seven o'clock while the grown-ups had their late dinner.

From the upper windows of our house we could see miles of open country lying below, with fields and a few straggling houses. One large meadow was fenced in to mark the bounds of the local cricket club. During our stay one match of some importance took place there. Whether or not it was for charity I do not know, but several tents and a large marquee were put up and the field was made gay with flags. They charged a shilling to go in, children half-price. Father took us boys and we sat on the grass and watched what was my first cricket match. Among the players were the redoubtable Dr W. G. and the Read brothers, W. W. and Maurice. It was pleasant sitting on the grass and watching the game, but I nearly went to sleep.

The thing that I enjoyed most at Wimbledon was walking across the Common to the rifle-butts. On a Saturday afternoon, when the red flag was hoisted, I would watch the shooting, sneaking up as close as I dared to the firing-point. Some of the riflemen wore Volunteer uniforms and were using Martini-Henry rifles. (Readers of *Drawn*

from Memory will remember that I knew quite a lot about guns.) It was fun to listen for the bullet hitting the iron target – 'Whang!' On off days I could explore the butts and inspect the dents on the targets and perhaps pick up a flattened leaden bullet or even a brass cartridge-case.

Once a week our household trooped to the bottom of the garden after the evening meal. The Aunts were muffled up and we waited in the growing darkness for the firework display at the Crystal Palace. Though we had only a distant view, it was an impressive sight, for which I was given a special dispensation to stay up late.

I did not go back to London with the others at the end of August. I had been invited to stay with Father's cousins in Guildford. Great-Uncle Richard had built a house on Guildown, and his daughter, my cousin Marion, lived there with her aunt. This aunt, Georgina Warren by name, was a great character of unknown antiquity, for she was always at pains to keep her age secret. When the time for

the census came along she would pack herself off for the night to a friend of presumably the same age as herself; this friend alone knew the truth. Great-Aunt Georgina was in charge of the livestock at Guildown, but never would admit that chickens grew up. She kept a large square basket with a trap-door at the side for them to roost in. As they regarded this as their home from an early age they would go in there to roost when almost fully grown. The gardener tried to point out that this meant overcrowding, but Aunt Georgie was adamant. 'They have always been there,' she argued. Finally the lid of the basket was unfastened in her presence, and layers of chickens were disclosed, the luckless ones at the bottom nearly suffocated.

Then there was the matter of wine. The old lady said that she could not bear the taste of it, but always seemed willing to make quite sure by trial. She would shake her head and say 'No! You know I don't like it.' Then: 'Well, perhaps I'll have just a taste.' The glass would be poured out and she would take a sip. Another shake of the head and 'No, I don't like it.' After a pause it would be noticed that the glass was empty. Then: 'Try a little more, Aunt Georgy,' and a little more would be tried.

She was an indefatigable gardener, and I spent a large part of my time following her round and learning the names of the flowers and when seeds should, or should not, be sown. She had a cat called Agnes and in the evening after dinner Aunt Georgie would sit on her special chair with Agnes on her lap; half-asleep, she would clean the cat's ears with a hairpin.

The thought of going to school at 'Oliver's', as St John's Wood Preparatory School was called, bore heavily upon me as the end of the summer holidays approached. I felt self-conscious in my black clothes, which did not fit at all well. The knickerbockers were too long and became known at school as 'Shepard Secundus's three-quarter bags'. I was also ashamed of my hat, a horrid round thing with a small peak. When the dread day arrived Cyril and I trotted off to Gower Street Station on the Underground and changed trains at Baker Street. From the platform I cast longing eyes upwards to the walls of the primary school where I had spent four happy years.

Chapter Two

OLIVER'S

OLIVER'S was halfway along Acacia Road on the north side. Two stone gateposts gave on to a weedy drive, which in turn led to a gravelled playground. Across the corner stood the school house, square and forbidding. It might well have been a prison; all it lacked was a notice over the door: 'Abandon hope, all ye that enter here'. This academy for young gentlemen was run by

two 'Heads': Mr Oliver, with a mortar-board tilted forward on his forehead and an ever-present cane, and Mr Jones, a quiet bearded fellow who sometimes took the top class. There were two assistant masters: one, Tucker by name, was known as 'Tommy', a kindly man and a contrast to the other, Payne, a young man with a personality far from being calculated to inspire confidence in the young.

Our days were spent in trying to avoid punishment. If this did not come from Oliver or Payne, then it was dealt out in full measure in the playground, where it was the custom for small fry to be chased around, herded together, and then made to run the gauntlet of the bigger boys' lethal weapons made from elastic and called 'Tollywags'. Sometimes catapults were aimed at us, and on occasion even an airgun fired at our legs. The journey home had its perils too. For there was perpetual warfare between the school and the local errand boys. It became usual for us to proceed as far as we were able in convoy. Woe betide the youngster caught alone! He was pelted with stones or mud, and after defending himself as best he could with his school satchel, often had to take refuge in a shop in the High Street.

I do not remember learning anything at Oliver's beyond an apprenticeship in self-preservation. It happened in the playground one day after some unusually savage bullying that a small boy named Puente, who was half Spanish, became slightly hysterical. I think this rather frightened the offenders, for they melted away. I got very worked up, for Puente was a friend of mine, and I made up my mind that something must be done. Hardly aware of what I was doing, I cornered one of the bullies, and, tears streaming down my face, poured forth a torrent of protest. He looked very surprised and wanted to know what it was all about. He was really a decent chap and didn't smack my head and tell me to mind my own business, but listened patiently while I became more coherent in my plea for the underdog. 'What's your name?' he asked. I told him. Then to my surprise he said: 'You kids should show fight. Use your fists. Look here, I'll show you how.' There and then he gave me a lesson in boxing, telling me how to keep my thumbs tucked in. I promptly passed this on, rather cockily, to my fellow sufferers. I should like

to be able to say that from that
day all bullying ceased, but it
would hardly be a statement of
fact.

I do not know when the
school building was erected or
for what purpose. There was an
old white house alongside, where
the Head resided, and the house
must at one time have been a
home with a drive and extensive
grounds. The school hall was a
big room with a great iron stove
and windows high up which
rumour said had once been a

chapel. There was a platform at the far end backed by a wooden
partition and the walls were matchboarding below with white-
wash above. Lockers ran along one side. Junior classes were held
at each end of this hall, while Mr Oliver took a senior class in
a smaller room at the back. I remained among the small fry
all the time I was there, thus achieving the ambition of every boy
to be as inconspicuous as possible. There was a football team, and
I believe it occasionally played a match, but as our ground was
gravelled, very little could be done there and games were usually
played out at Neasden. It was not till I went to St Paul's that I began
to take an interest in football.

That Autumn term seemed endless, but towards the end things
brightened up when it was announced that the school was to produce
the trial scene from 'Pickwick' before the Christmas holidays.
Rehearsing for this meant a busy time for the elder boys who had

parts. I had faint hopes that I might get slipped in amongst the jurymen, but I was too small. Cyril, however, was luckier, and I always wanted to stay behind with him to watch the rehearsals. This had the added advantage of avoiding going home alone. Though I do not suppose that any boys in the school were over

fourteen, they seemed to an undersized creature like myself very big and imposing when they stood up and declaimed their lines. The boy who played Winkle was a huge success. He had a natural stammer combined with a vacant expression, and his genuine efforts to give his name in court, 'W-W-W-Winkle', brought the house down. There was no scenery, nor were there any costumes, which I considered rather spoilt the effect.

We did much better in that respect at home in Gordon Square, when we produced a composite pantomime introducing Cinderella and other well-known characters. The whole was written and directed by Ethel, who had a genius for both writing and story-telling. Our cousins, Violet and Stanley, and two or three younger children were roped in, and though there was little chance of rehearsing, for they lived far away in Kensington, the parts were written out, and it was hoped that they might be learnt. In the event the script was brought on to the stage and constantly referred to. We were allowed to improvise some scenery in the back drawing-room with screens and curtains. The lighting left much to be desired, with a gas chandelier hanging from the ceiling in the centre. Also there was no curtain, the large double doors having to serve the purpose. As it was winter, we could not open the sash-window on to the balcony and so give an excuse for a woodland scene, but we achieved a most convincing firelight effect with a large lamp fitted with a red glass shade like a glorified strawberry.

Seated before this, Cinderella, in scene two, was discovered pining for the ball. Cyril was the Prince and I played several parts, but most of my time was spent in changing costumes and fixing up the 'scenery'. Ethel alone knew her words; in fact, she knew all our words too and was able to prompt. As we all dried up sooner or later she had to fill in a good many blanks. Violet, as the Fairy Godmother, suffered from stage fright, and after her opening sentence, 'Why are you crying, Cinderella?' incontinently fled behind a screen without waiting for the answer. The audience was composed of our Aunts, our cousin from Guildford, who was staying in the house, and, seated on high chairs at the back, the maids. Father, having had some experience of our theatricals, had provided himself with an evening paper. However, we children all enjoyed it immensely and had a grand supper afterwards down in the dining-room.

Cyril and I each had a birthday in December – too near Christmas for our liking, as one present often did duty for both festivals. 'With love from . . . for birthday and Christmas' was, we considered, not playing the game. But we did not do at all badly, for no Aunt could overlook the two anniversaries while we were living in their house. My Godmother, Aunt Alicia, gave me a conjuring set for my birthday, a real slap-up affair with some very ingenious tricks in it, and we felt that this called for a special performance. The set contained instructions on how to arrange a show with an accomplice hidden from the audience. We borrowed a small table such as a conjuror would use and draped it with a gay tablecloth. In this

confined space I, being the
smallest, hid myself, and
there I had to remain
concealed till the double
doors closed upon the
scene. Ethel acted as conjuror with wand (pro-
vided with the set) and
top-hat (provided by
Father). She placed the
hat on the table brim
downwards, having first
shown it to be empty.
Then, 'Hey, presto!' a
wave of the wand, the
hat was lifted, and there
lay a silver watch (bor-

rowed from Aunt Annie's nurse). Ethel was adept at distracting
the attention of the audience while my small fumbling hands reached
up from behind and placed the object under the hat. I had a small
collection of articles down there in the dark – a coin, a playing-card,
an old snuff-box – and all Ethel had to do was to say: 'And what
shall we find now? I think it will be a coin of the realm,' and lo
and behold it was! With Cyril, she essayed a thought-reading act,
but this had to be carefully rehearsed and was quite beyond me.

We looked forward to Christmas with mixed feelings. It would
be the first we had spent without Mother, but Father and our aunts
did their utmost to make it as happy a time as possible. Aunt Fanny
took us shopping at Shoolbred's in the Tottenham Court Road, and
we bought cards at the stationers in Torrington Place. Then there

were the barrows in the back streets where we bought holly and mistletoe. I had saved up nearly ten shillings and decided that I would buy Father a really good present. I spent hours debating what it should be and pestering Ethel and Cyril for advice on the subject. What I finally bought was a silver toothpick, price four and sixpence. It was a dainty little thing that slid in and out like a pencil-holder, but I do not think it was much good to Father, for I never saw him use it.

Christmas Day brought excitement and the opening of presents. We all went to St Pancras Church in the morning and were allowed to sit up for late dinner. This was a grand feast, with crackers and crystallized fruits, almonds and raisins. There was an enormous turkey which Father carved, and a blazing plum pudding; moreover, the pudding had new sixpenny-pieces in it and each child somehow found one in his or her helping. Before dinner we sat in the back drawing-room and sang carols to Ethel's accompaniment. The only blot on the day was that such a rich dinner called

for a dose. At bedtime I had to sit up while Aunt Fanny handed me two small pills. I made a great show of swallowing them, but I am afraid they were slipped under the bed while her back was turned. Consulting Cyril next day, I found that he too had taken evasive action. Neither of us was any the worse.

A few days before we went back to school Father told us that he had decided that we must have a home of our own. He had been looking for a house, something that he could afford to rent, and had found one in Hammersmith. It seemed a very remote place to me, but it had the attraction of being on the river, which meant that it would be near the University Boat Race. What he did not tell us then was the fact that he had been consulting our Uncle Willie, who was his elder brother and a master at St Paul's, as to our becoming pupils there. There had been some talk of this before, but with all the changes in our lives we had given up hope of its ever happening.

We were delighted at the thought of once again having our own home and eagerly asked Father to let us see the house. So one afternoon we all set forth by train to Hammersmith, boarded a horse-tram at the Broadway, and alighted at Ravenscourt Park.

Theresa Terrace stood on the opposite side of the road to the Park and next to Beavor Lane. It was a terrace of Georgian houses, built, in pairs, of London Stock bricks about a hundred and sixty years ago. There was a narrow strip of green in front surrounded by posts and chains, much in the style that can still be seen in Chiswick and the Mall. The house, No. 2, had three stories and a basement with area railings. There was a portico over the front door topped by a balcony with iron railings. The front door, wide and square, had a fanlight over it. Inside was a stone-flagged hall. It was a most attractive house, as indeed were all the houses on that terrace, and Father told us that there was a nice garden at the back with a studio. Moreover, the rent was only fifty pounds a year, an important point, since Father's finances were in a bad way. The tenants were an old artist and his wife, who showed us over the house. I think they were sad at leaving the place, as it had been their home for many years. The artist told us that his next-door neighbour was Stacpoole, the engraver, while farther up the Terrace had been the home of George Mason, the painter, and at the end lived Gleason White. Only a short distance away was Beavor Lodge, the home of W. B. Richmond, the Royal Academician.

The view from the upper rooms of our house was quite countrified. Adjoining Ravenscourt Park were the grounds of Hamlet House, and acres of market gardens filled with fruit trees stretched all the way to Young's corner and beyond.

Father told us that it would be some time before we could move into the house, for even when the artist and his wife had vacated it there would be much work for the builders and decorators. He planned to add on a bathroom and small bedroom at the side, and all the rooms needed repapering and the woodwork painting. He was particularly pleased with a fireplace in the drawing-room, though it had a dreadful overmantel with wooden shelves. The mantelpiece itself and the sides were fluted white marble. A medallion at each corner had a lotus pattern in the centre. He said it was a fine example of late Georgian work. Another thing that pleased him was a pair of tall mahogany bookcases built into recesses flanking the fireplace. Being an architect, Father naturally valued such things. It was a great many years before I learned to appreciate them too. These bookcases, saved from the house-breakers when the house was demolished, now ornament my own drawing-room.

The Aunts were very distressed at the thought of our going so far away, but they realized what it meant to us to have a home of our own and did all they could to help. They had been told of the plan for Cyril and me to go to St Paul's School, and they appreciated that we should benefit by being near the School. Meanwhile, we were still in the dark about all this and could only look forward to more dreary terms at 'Oliver's'. Relief, however, was to come sooner than we expected.

Chapter Three

THERESA TERRACE

PERHAPS because Cyril and I had become used to the life, the Easter term at Oliver's did not seem so bad. The thought of moving to a house of our own, with a garden, gave us a lot to talk about and we made all sorts of plans. What pleased us as much as anything was the knowledge that we were to sleep together in the upstairs bedroom, whence we could look out on to the high road and see the horse-trams going by. Cyril was now nearly a head taller than I and was no longer an object for bullying. I benefited from this, for I could always rely upon his intervening on my behalf. We boasted the titles of 'Shepard Primus' and 'Shepard Secundus' and trouble stopped when Primus came to the aid of Secundus.

It was Aunt Emily who let the cat out of the bag about our going to St Paul's. One Sunday, Uncle Willie came to tea at Gordon Square, and Aunt Emily in spite of nudges from her sisters asked him at the tea-table whether we should be in his class. Father saved the situation by saying: 'There, boys, it's out. Are you glad?' To judge by our expressions no answer was required, but it was not until we were alone in the study that we gave full vent to our feelings. Uncle Willie came in to us before he left and told us something about the school, warning us that we should have to spend several terms at the St Paul's preparatory school, Colet Court, before moving up to the big school. This did not, however, damp our spirits. In the light of my subsequent knowledge of Father's financial state at the time,

I am quite sure that Uncle Willie had arranged for us to be taken at reduced fees, otherwise Father could not have afforded it. Nothing mattered now; we were going to be real Public School boys, and didn't we let them know it at Oliver's! We became the envy of the smaller boys and were dubbed 'lucky young swine' by the elder ones.

I don't know how long Oliver's continued after we left. To me it soon became no more than an unpleasant memory. But, years afterwards, when I was a student at the Royal Academy Schools, the student at the next easel was Denis Eden, who had been at Oliver's with me, and we some-times talked of the school. He turned to me one day and said in a low voice, 'Shepard, do you ever wake up in the morning with a feeling you have to go back to that place?' I am sure it had a blighting effect on both our young lives.

It was a great relief to us, as I am sure it must have been to the grown-ups, to be able to talk openly about the future. I felt that I ought to go into long trousers, as Cyril had already done; my 'threequarter bags'

C

were a continuous source of shame; but relief was denied me and I had to wear the wretched things for several more terms.

Our greatest treat at this time was to be taken to Hammersmith by Father to see how the builders were getting on at Theresa Terrace. There was a pile of slates stacked outside and the hall was full of timber. Upstairs the walls were being stripped and the woodwork painted. Cyril and I clattered up and down the stairs into every room and down to the basement, where the scullery floor was being relaid. The garden was rather a wilderness, but we all got to work on the weeds, and rescued clumps of flags and other plants. There was a grape-vine on the house wall, and a lovely Morello cherry-tree coming into bloom at the end. The studio had been a stable. It had been properly floored and a north light added. A door at the back gave on to a lane, and an old stove was being replaced by an anthracite burner from Pither's in Mortimer Street. We were allowed to choose the wallpaper for our own bedrooms. Ethel chose blue, and we boys took a long time to make up our minds, finally settling for a spotted paper that I was never quite sure about. The work seemed to progress with agonizing slowness, but it was finished at last, and in the Easter holidays we were able to take our two younger Aunts to see our new home. Aunt Fanny, ever practical, closely inspected the kitchen fireplace, and was not very complimentary about our choice of bedroom wallpaper. Aunt Emily complained that the stairs were steep; in fact, she was breathless when she got to the top and quite failed to see that the view from our window was enhanced by the horse-trams. However, it was a fine day, the sun was shining and the Morello cherry was in full bloom, and that, they agreed, was a very lovely sight.

The great day came when the furniture arrived. It had been stored in a depository and was very dusty. We all helped to carry

The Morello cherry was in full bloom

in the smaller things, Father giving us directions as to where to put them. I do not know how they managed to get the piano up the narrow stairs, but somehow it reached the drawing-room, after the carpet had been laid. We spent the first night camping on mattresses after having a picnic supper of bread and jam and cocoa. The next day, to our great joy, our dear Lizzie arrived in a four-wheeler. She had been with us ever since I could remember, and before that too,

for she had been Mother's nurse, and when Father and Mother were married came to them as cook. She brought her cat in a basket and he had to be kept in for several days to get used to the place. She promptly took us out to find the most promising local tradesmen. There was plenty of choice in the High Road. It was exciting to see the postman arrive with letters, including one from the Aunts with love and good wishes for happiness in our new home.

Cyril and I had one more term at Oliver's, but the end was in sight. We knew that we were to go to Colet Court in September. For the summer holidays we did not feel we wanted to go anywhere, but the Aunts had taken a house at St Leonards and wanted us to join them, and Father said that they would be very disappointed if we did not go. So it was arranged we should spend four weeks with them. Father, meanwhile, was to go to Normandy for a painting trip. He had always made a hobby of painting in water-colours, and would settle down with his easel and white umbrella to paint what he called 'A nice little bit'. This usually consisted of a church or some picturesque cottage. So we saw him off armed with his traps.

The house at St Leonards was called Rosemount and stood above the Archery Gardens. Cyril and I found plenty to amuse us down on the beach. We were now old enough to go out alone, and sometimes we forgot the passage of time, and arrived home late for midday dinner. We were not allowed to bathe alone. Bathing was rather a formal proceeding. Aunt Fanny or Aunt Emily would accompany us, carrying their voluminous bathing-dresses strapped in a towel. They would choose a machine, which they would share with Ethel, while Cyril and I scrambled into another. We could not swim, but were taken to the sea-water baths on Hastings Front and given lessons. The instructor fastened a rope round our middles and then made us jump from the diving-board. Ethel made light of this, but I would stand shivering on the board, urged on by cries of encouragement from aunts and instructor, till finally a tightening of the rope forced me in. Coming to the surface, I floundered frantically to the steps, deaf to the shouts of 'Take it slowly!'

Father was in Normandy for a fortnight, and he brought back sketches of Lisieux, Honfleur and Rouen. He told us about the cathedral there and the lovely Normandy churches, and how he had spent two nights at a little *auberge* with sanded floors where wine

Stand shivering on the board

was less than one franc a bottle. One day when he could afford it, he promised, we should all go there.

Ethel was now a pupil at Queen's College, Harley Street, and was miles ahead of us boys in learning. She was reading Ruskin and we got rather tired of hearing him quoted on all occasions. She was having piano lessons at the London Academy, where I went with my violin once a week. I had to stand up and play before Herr Politzer and was then handed over to Miss Salmond, very patient and, what was more important to me, very good looking. I studied there for three years, but I never found time for practising and made little progress. Before I left St Paul's I gave up music for good.

There was plenty to do in our new home, but Cyril and I found time to go exploring round the neighbourhood. We would slip out of the back studio door into the lane. It was unmetalled and very muddy and we had to pick our way past the high walls of Beavor Lodge. There was a factory at the bottom of the lane by the river. Here we could turn either to the right or to the left; we preferred the right as it led towards Chiswick and the barges, their red sails furled, lying on the mud opposite the Eyot. We liked studying the old houses, Walpole House in particular, and would then go as far

We speculated on the size of her guns

as Chiswick Old Church, with the little inn alongside and Thorneycroft's the shipbuilders. A new type of torpedo-boat called a Destroyer had just been built and was being fitted out in the river. We speculated on the size of her guns and came to the conclusion that the one to be placed on the fo'c'sle would be a twelve-pounder. A waterman told us that she could steam at nearly twenty knots. Later we were to see the 'Speedy', a torpedo-gunboat, quite a large vessel for the river.

Every Sunday Father took us to church at Chiswick. I went very willingly as I knew I should see something of interest lying off

Thorneycroft's. After church we would walk back with the Calthrops, who were old friends of Father's. Claude Calthrop, an outstanding painter who had barely reached middle age, had died recently, leaving a widow and two children, Everard and Hope.

Everard was several years older than us. He had been to St Paul's, but had left before we entered the school. He was at that time a cadet at Woolwich, learning to be a Gunner at the 'Shop'. He was a very clever draughtsman and would certainly have made his name as an artist. He had a brilliant career in the Artillery, where he made a special study of Eastern warfare, learned Chinese and Japanese and became Military Attaché at Tokyo. The Calthrops' house was on the Mall, close to Hammersmith Bridge; it was a charming old house with a glass-covered verandah on the first floor. It was from here that in the following year I was to see my first Boat Race. We had a struggle to reach the house, for the crowd was thick by the Bridge and the public house close by was overflowing. Among the throng were men selling favours, light or dark blue, some made of paper and others of dyed straw costing a penny. More expensive ones were fashioned like birds. Everyone seemed to be wearing his or her fancied colour. When the race started the sound of cheering could

be heard along the banks, gradually coming nearer until the boats shot under Hammersmith Bridge and came in sight. On this occasion, to my joy, it was a Dark Blue boat that appeared first.

Dion Clayton Calthrop was Everard's cousin and was often at

41

their house. He was a son of John Clayton, the actor, and Nina
Boucicault. He, too, had been at St Paul's and was now studying at
St John's Wood Art School. He asked me if I wanted to be an artist.
When I said yes, he told me that it was a precarious life and badly
paid, but all the same, he was going in for it and it was jolly well
worth while.

We often went to see the Calthrops, and when Everard was there
he would talk to me about art and artists. He had been studying the
French Impressionists. Now, I had heard about these fellows from
some of Father's artist friends, those who painted in water-colour and
would sit round and condemn what they called 'slipshod work'.
The pains they themselves took to produce, year after year, the same
kind of subject with the same dull colouring were rewarded by a
ready sale. The galleries were filled, and on the opening day dealers
would compete and sometimes buy up a whole wall of pictures,
taking the bad with the good.

I listened to such remarks as 'Might as well paint a pair of old
boots' or 'The fellow paints a field of mustard – *mustard!* – and has
the cheek to call it a picture.' I just listened and wondered. Father's
great friend Frank Dicksee, with all his academic training and in spite
of his being a Royal Academician, never spoke in such terms and was
far more catholic in his tastes. It was years before I was to make
acquaintance with the Impressionists, years spent in painstaking study
of the antique, a cautious introduction to painting. Frank encouraged
me in this by allowing me to try my hand with oils. I sat for him on
several occasions at his studio in Peel Street, and, the sitting over, he
would give me a palette and brushes and set up a vase or some
bottles. Working on a piece of canvas board, I would quickly get
into trouble, but dabbled on quite content and feeling I was being a
real artist. We often spent Sunday afternoon and evening with the

Dicksees in their house in Fitzroy Square. Frank's sister Margaret, whom we all called Minnie, was also an artist, and an illustrator too. She had a studio on the first floor in their house. Their father, Thomas Dicksee, had recently died, and they were looking out for a new home farther out of London. Now that I was old enough to stay on for supper, it was a great treat to meet so many musical and artistic people and to hear what was happening in the great world.

On one side of Fitzroy Square was the headquarters of a Volunteer Fusilier regiment. From the Dicksees' window on a Sunday afternoon we could watch the men mustering, streaming out of the building, adjusting busbies and accoutrements. Then the band would appear and strike up, and off they would all march, followed by a crowd of sightseers, the music gradually dying away in the distance. I decided that if I could not be a soldier, I might at least be a Volunteer.

We travelled home by train from Portland Road to Hammer-smith. Walking along King Street on a Sunday or Saturday night was not a pleasant experience; there were too many 'drunks' about. The public-houses were open till midnight and each was filled with a noisy crowd which overflowed on to the pavement. It was a pathetic sight to see a woman, often with a baby in her arms, patiently waiting outside to guide her man home. Fights were not infrequent, and we had to take side-turnings to avoid them. Sunday was a dreary day in London. It was no wonder so many people found solace in the pubs. Saturday night was quite a different matter; then the shops were open until very late and did a roaring trade. Jim Burrows, 'the Butcher King' as he called himself, stood outside his shop selling off his meat. He had a stentorian voice and a ready wit and kept up a running commentary on the choiceness of his wares. There was a rival shop opposite and prices were cut first by one and then by the other, with the crowds dodging backwards and forwards to get the best bargains.

It was some time later that I learned that the astute Mr Burrows owned both shops and staged this mock rivalry for his own advantage.

Jim Burrows, the Butcher King

Chapter Four

BEWSHER'S

IN a state of intense excitement Cyril and I set off for our first day at Colet Court. We walked all the way: along King Street, the Broadway, then past the hospital, to come in sight of the big red school standing back from the road. Its gold-faced clock would tell us if we had plenty of time or must hurry. 'Bewsher's', as Colet Court was called, stood opposite, red like its big brother but not so imposing. Along with other new boys we were lined up and inspected by 'Jimmy' Bewsher, the Head Master. We were allotted to classes and were told to go to the office 'in the break' to be fitted with our school caps. There was no school uniform, but we were warned that gay ties must not be worn. I felt very small and followed the excellent principle of making myself as inconspicuous as possible. In the break we got our caps, dark blue with a white Maltese Cross, and found ourselves the object of the interest of some of the older boys. 'What's your name?' 'How old are you?' 'What's your father?' 'Where have you been to school?' No one seemed to have heard of Oliver's. There was no suspicion

of bullying and the masters were quite a different type from what
we had been used to.

After school we walked home with a boy called Broad. He had
been at Bewsher's several terms and was rather condescending, but
he gave us a lot of useful advice. He lived at Stamford Brook, and
later I got to know him well. The eldest of a large family of brothers
and sisters, his parents had a comfortable white house called Stamford
Brook Lodge with a garden facing the Green. He was the same age
as myself but nearly as big as Cyril and told me that I ought to be
in long trousers, which to me was like rubbing salt into an open
wound.

I was terribly ashamed of my Christian name and had blurted it
out under questioning. This, he said, was a cardinal error, and laid
me open to any amount of chaff. ' "*Ernest*"! Fancy being called
that!' followed by loud laughter. How I wished that I were George
or William, or just John as he was.

Lizzie had tea ready for us when we reached home and was eager
to know how we liked our new school. We were able to tell her that
it promised well and had a nice big playground. I drew a map of this
for her, showing where the wash-houses were and the asphalt piece
at the end with the giant stride in the middle. I told her how relieved
I was to find several other boys in knickerbockers. We showed her
our school caps and told her which classes we had been put into. We
had taken sandwiches for our lunch, and when Father came in he
asked us if we would mind doing this every day, as having our meal
in the dining-hall at school would come expensive.

School began with Morning Prayers and a Hymn in the Big
Hall, and as I had a good treble voice it was not long before I found
myself in the school choir. The winter game was Soccer and I
became quite keen on this, kicking a ball about with other small

Meet in the Broads' summer-house

boys in the luncheon hour. I did not find the work too hard at
first, but could never get ahead with Latin or Greek, which was a

handicap when, later on, I got into the higher forms. Drawing classes were dull; we were given cubes and cylinders to draw and shade; and it was not till I moved on to the Big School that I was able to let myself go in the drawing school.

We had not been at Bewsher's long before Broad invited us to tea on a half-holiday. With his large garden and several brothers and sisters this promised good fun. We started a sort of club, chiefly devoted to eating. We would spend our pocket-money on any delicacies we fancied, and then meet in the Broads' summer-house, pool our supplies, and make a feast of it. This was all very well, but it did not always come off. Funds were sometimes low, and then the younger Broads would raid their mother's store cupboard, and this led to trouble with the cook. On one occasion we found a shop in King Street selling off a job lot of sardines; we bought a dozen tins for two shillings and opened them in the summer-house. We thought they tasted a bit odd, and sure enough we had stomach-aches all round, and Mrs Broad dosed us with purgatives. We were always getting into trouble with the gardener, and I am not surprised, for we had no respect for the beds and would build huts among the shrubs, raiding the tool-shed to find any likely pieces of timber. The stable and coach-house had a loft above in which apples were stored. One of the younger boys found the key, but kept the fact dark until his elder brother caught him pocketing the apples. He was then arraigned as a traitor, the key was confiscated, and we older boys used it for our own satisfaction.

With a friend of the Broads, a little girl named Eva, I fell deeply in love. She lived in Sinclair Road and had two younger sisters. They were often at the Broads' house and we all played together in the garden. She was about my own age and John and I were rivals for her affections. I regret to say that he always cut me out.

It was the urge of love that led me to ask Father to let us join a dancing-class. This was held at a Dr Pope's near by, and once a week Ethel, Cyril and I would go there, carrying our dancing-shoes and, as far as I was concerned, cleaned up and dressed with the greatest care. Our teacher was a Miss Thompson, very small and dainty but wrinkled. She used a scent that I did not like, but it was a treat to

dance with her. She would call, 'Take your partners for the Barn Dance, please,' and a rush would be made for Eva. It was not often that I got there first, and when disappointed had to content myself with another, less attractive, partner. A young man played the piano: 'Tumptity-tumpity tum!' He had a wonderful head of hair, curled and pomaded. The class over, we would walk to the tram with the girls and their governess. When we parted I would live for next week. I chose a Christmas card for Eva with the greatest care. It was embellished with the most amorous verses, but it did not have any effect. The fact was that I was not a good dancer, and though I felt safe with a polka or barn dance, it took me a long time to master the waltz.

In November preparations were made for a big firework display in the school grounds and we were asked to bring along our own fireworks to augment it. Posts and wooden frameworks were erected and we all hoped for a fine night, but we were disappointed as it poured with rain and the display had to be put off. When it did take place a few nights later, the night was damp and foggy, and all our own fireworks had been expended. The display was not a success.

The Broads had grand parties at Stamford Brook Lodge at Christmas time. We were given the free run of the house, and their cousin, who was a professional entertainer, amused us for hours. He had one pet song:

> *Oh, Susannah! Don't you cry for me!*
> *I come from Alabama with me banjo on me knee.*

Our favourite verse finished like this:

> *A piece of cake was in her eye,*
> *A tear was in her mouth,*
> *And Oh, Susannah! Don't you cry!*
> *For I'm coming from de South.*

There was plenty of snow that winter and we had properly organized snowball-fights, 'Oxford' versus 'Cambridge', led by two masters named Sankey and Brownjohn (Sankey afterwards became Lord Chancellor). I won my first prize ever at the end of that term. It was, of course, for drawing, for in nothing else did I shine. The prize was *Tom Brown's Schooldays* with the original illustrations. I read it with joy and have done so frequently since. Soon after that

a move brought me into Skinner's form, Lower Ist A. We earned distinction at football by winning the class 'sixes', the games being played with six a side. The final, with Lower Ist B, was a hard-fought battle. Skinner and MacDougal, the Form Masters, were as excited as any one. We just got home by a goal. Bridges, our goal-keeper, was one of the heroes of the match. He was a dour stopper. I played back with Douglas Home. Skinner let us off all homework for three days.

I had two terms in Skinner's and then, to my surprise, was moved to the top class, the Upper First. My time there was a happy one. We had a master called Botting who, besides being a good teacher, was a cheerful nice fellow. My particular friend in Upper First was William Temple: 'Fatty' we called him. He and I were always at different ends of the class in weekly lists, and I need not say which end I occupied, though on one occasion I did soar above him, much to his surprise. His father, then Bishop of London, had confirmed me. Temple left Bewsher's at the same time as I did, to go to Rugby. I wished at the time that he could have gone to St Paul's with me, but it would have made little difference if he had, for he was on the

Classical side while I was on the Science. I think he was always keen to follow his father into the Church. As a boy of thirteen he had a most forthright character and a grand sense of humour. He was, I believe, a few months younger than I.

With the coming of summer our aunts invited us to spend part of our holidays with them at the seaside. This year it was to be East-bourne, where they had taken a house in Enys Road; we joined them for three weeks in August. What I remember best about that visit is being taken to see the All-England Lawn Tennis Tournament in Devonshire Park. The play was something quite different from what I was accustomed to see on the lawns of our friends. Though the ladies' dresses were equally conventional, their standard of play was, to me, astonishingly higher. I saw Renshaw win the men's singles, and the Baddeley brothers knock everyone out in the doubles. The ladies served underarm, and though handicapped by long skirts, tight waists and high-necked blouses, managed to skip about the court exceedingly nimbly. The mixed doubles was won by Mrs and Mr Hillyard – I put them in that order for it was evident that she was the senior partner; any mishit by Mr Hillyard was the subject of muttered abuse from Mrs Hillyard; I sat quite near and heard it all. I had not realized before this that lawn tennis could provoke such strong feelings.

Some days later we went fishing with Father's boatman-friend of a previous year. On that earlier occasion the party had narrowly escaped destruction at the hands of the Sussex Volunteer Artillery engaged in target practice at a buoy out at sea. On this occasion our only danger was when Aunt Emily caught her first fish and nearly upset the boat in her excitement.

My brother Cyril left Bewsher's a year or so before I did, and although we continued to make the morning journey together, the

big school finished an hour later than Bewsher's. In the evening we did our homework together in the back study overlooking the garden, helped by our tame magpie. He lived in a cage, but as the door was never shut he was always hopping in and out and would peck about on the table and pick up any small object. This bird loved hiding things, and once he upset the inkpot over my prep. In the warm weather we would carry his cage into the garden and there he ruled supreme. Though we kept his wings clipped, he would chase all the birds, and woe betide any cat that ventured over the wall. He was after it in no time, chattering and flapping his stumpy wings. The only cat he did not chase was Lizzie's, between whom and himself there seemed to be an armed truce.

Christmas was like old times. The buying and sending of Christmas cards **and** such small presents as we could afford with our very limited pocket money added to the enjoyment of our holiday. We

paid our annual visit to Uncle Willie at his home in Kensington and came home the richer by five shillings apiece (two shining new half-crowns). After supper we were taken to Olympia to see a stirring military display called 'Chitral', with plenty of red-coated infantry storming cardboard heights. This was followed by a very realistic 'Derby Day'. The arena was filled with vehicles of all sorts from four-in-hands to donkey-carts. Finally we had a real race with jockeys, race-horses, bookies and all – not forgetting the welsher bookie who made off and was chased by the crowd.

A few days before Christmas we went shopping in King Street. I thought the lighted shops and the kerb lined with barrows wonderful. These barrows were lit by naphtha flares, dangerous-looking things which frequently went wrong and belched black smoke. All sorts of fruit could be bought, apples, oranges, pineapples and grapes. Roast chestnuts, hot potatoes and pomegranates were a penny each. Oyster barrows, lit by candles stuck in inverted bottles, were very popular. A man in dirty pink tights did a juggling act, helped by a small boy whom he balanced on his shoulders while tossing up shiny balls which the child caught. This all finished with a posture and a smirk. The boy then went round with a hat. I did not envy him; he must have been very cold in his little tights.

Farther up King Street the 'Butcher King' was in full blast, his shop-front hung with turkeys of all sizes. We watched these being sold off, competition with the shop opposite being as lively as ever.

It was long past my bedtime when we arrived home and Cyril and I stood looking out of our top-floor window. The trams had stopped, but in the faint light of the gas-lamps we could see the carts carrying fruit and vegetables from the market-gardens at Acton to Covent Garden. The horses plodded slowly along; they knew their way blindfold, which was just as well, for the drivers, wrapped in sacks, would certainly be asleep. The glow over King Street died down, but the voice of Jim Burrows could still be heard in the distance and somewhere a barrel-organ ground out the notes of 'The Lost Chord'.

The Aunts had given us a turkey and boxes of crystallized fruits, figs and dates. We peeled almonds, and on Christmas afternoon arranged the fruit with crackers around. Lizzie cooked a glorious pudding, and we all helped to lay the table and carry the dishes up from the kitchen. Esther and Mary Ann, Lizzie's two sisters, were below to keep her company and help with the disposal of a bottle of port wine that Father provided for them – Esther correct as ever in her black kid gloves which she never seemed to remove. After dinner Father read to us. He was a very good reader and had taken us through most of Dickens and some Walter Scott, but on this occasion I found myself dropping off to sleep.

Chapter Five

A COLD WINTER

IT turned very cold after Christmas and I suffered accordingly. Wearing knickerbockers, as I did, with rather rough worsted stockings, the icy winds chapped my ankles and knees, and as I never could find my gloves, my hands suffered also. I must have had a sensitive skin, for neither Ethel nor Cyril seemed to experience the same trouble. I had been set some form of holiday task and the best place to do it was in the kitchen, where it was always warm and cosy. In the back study where we usually worked there was only a small fire and we had to crouch over it to keep warm. After supper there was a much larger fire in the drawing-room, and we sat in front of this as long as we could. Father dozed in his chair and did not mark the passage of time. Suddenly he would wake up, look at his watch and exclaim: 'Look at the time, boys! You ought to have been in bed an hour ago! Off you go at once and no talking!' It did not take us long to undress and tumble shivering into our cold beds.

To add to our troubles this year our pipes froze, even the main pipe in the terrace. The Water Works man who came to see to things said that the main was too near the surface and he put up a stand-pipe for us. We endured the same discomforts we had experienced four years earlier at Kent Terrace, when we had to fill the bath with water carried in cans and jugs from outside. Our bedroom was always cold. The water in the washstand jug generally froze in the

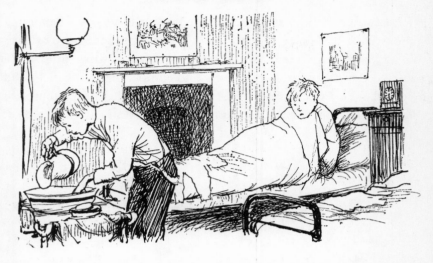

night, so that getting up in the morning by gas-light was a penance. Repeated shouts from below failed to move us until Lizzie rang the breakfast-bell. The poor horses pulling the trams had a bad time. They could not start until sand had been thrown down, and even then they would snort and steam in the cold air.

We had one great treat during the holidays. Father took us to a Christmas pantomime at the Crystal Palace. We travelled by train and arrived before midday to have dinner in a restaurant where we were served by a waiter in a very grubby white shirt. The dinner was a grand one—grilled chops, nice big ones, washed down with glasses of cider. The pantomime in the afternoon was not so elaborate as the one I had seen at Drury Lane three years before, but for me was nevertheless unforgettable on account of Cissy Loftus, who played the Principal Boy's part. Not only could she mimic and sing to perfection, she was so gay, and no male boy ever had such lovely legs! Father bought us a pictorial programme with a photograph of her. I cut it out and kept it for years. Afterwards we saw a **Panorama** in a circular building in the grounds. It represented the siege of **Paris** in 1870, reconstructed by a famous French battle-painter. We entered a small tower in the centre and climbed up to a gallery and from there looked all round on the scene of battle in the suburbs of Paris during one of the sorties. It was so realistic I could almost

Drawn at the Crystal Palace

imagine it to be the real thing. I had seen a similar panorama of the battle of Waterloo at the Aquarium in Westminster a year or two before, but this one was far better.

About this time Father arranged to share his studio with an artist named E. F. Brewtnall. Mr Brewtnall lived in Bedford Park, and his easel and some of his paintings arrived in a barrow. He was a member of the Royal Society of Painters in Water Colour, but spent much of his time painting sunsets in oils. I do not think he found a ready sale for these, and he was, I believe, quite as hard up as Father, but he was a good tenant and a kindly man. He would arrive about half-past nine in the morning, and if our magpie was out it would accompany him down the garden, pecking his trousers on the way. Brewtnall was a fellow member of a society of artists called 'The Anonymous', the members of which met on Thursday evenings at Frank Dicksee's studio. Each week a paper was read on a subject of topical interest. As one or two of the members were strong radicals some very heated discussions took place, Father told us.

There was a lot of unemployment at the time and small groups of men paraded the streets, chanting:

We've got no work to do-o-o,
We've got no work to do.
We are poor hungry lab'ring men
And we've got no work to do.

Sometimes the traffic had to stop while a procession went by carrying banners. We heard that there were meetings in Trafalgar Square which were followed by rioting. Dramatic pictures of it all appeared in the illustrated papers. It was a good thing when the hard weather broke, for the unemployed must have had a bad time with no money to buy firing for their homes. We, too, were thankful to see the last of it, and Lizzie could light the kitchen range again, for she had found it difficult to cook on a gas-ring.

It was some time in March that we received an invitation from my Aunt Ellen to stay with her in Sussex. She had delicate health and London did not agree with her, so she had decided, many years before, to leave her sisters in Gordon Square and, much against their advice, to live by herself in the country. It had turned out well, for she had found a Scots maid who became devoted to her and remained with her till her death thirty-five years later. The maid, Ganson, came from the Shetland Islands. She had strong views on religion and the evils of tobacco. The two lived at Steyning, and it was arranged that we were to go there in the Easter holidays. The house was one of a pair on the Bramber Road. It had a fine view of the Downs from the back, but was badly built of brick and flint and most unattractive to look at. It still stands, as ugly as ever. Aunt Ellen was very deaf and used an ear-trumpet, but as this was generally mislaid in the folds of her dress it was difficult to pitch one's voice so as to avoid startling her. There were two dogs, Dick and Jip, of indeterminate breed and growing fat from lack of exercise. There was also a strange pet, a young lamb, that lived in the garden. The little thing had been given by the next-door neighbour, an eccentric doctor called Clouting. For me, it was a most enchanting household, with the dogs and the lamb – all, I may say, on the best of terms – and Ganson ever solicitous for our welfare and providing the most delectable meals.

In the morning the lamb would greet us. It had a shed at the end of the garden, and when we called would come bounding towards us. We made it a little collar and took it out on the end of a rope, but Dr Clouting warned us to keep off the road because of stray dogs which might not be as friendly as Dick and Jip. We climbed through the fence at the top of the garden on to the Downs, where the lamb would skip about on the end of his long rope, and the dogs, glad to be out for a run, would hunt for rabbits in the hedges.

We found the Doctor most entertaining. He took us for walks and told us about the countryside. He had a bearded friend who sometimes joined us, a naturalist. He certainly knew all about birds, and was very quick at spotting them, but he carried a walking-stick gun and shot those with the brightest colouring, slipping them into a capacious inside pocket. I cannot help thinking it was the bright feathers he was after; there was a big demand for them at the time for the adornment of ladies' hats.

Father joined us for the week-end, and I realized how fortunate it was that he did not smoke, for Aunt Ellen, as well as Ganson, had a horror of it. The doctor next door was a confirmed pipe-smoker and my aunt complained to Father that the pernicious fumes from his pipe even penetrated into her house. Father, with his experience as an architect, started to investigate, and soon found the explanation. There was a wide crack in the brickwork between the two houses in one of the upstairs rooms. Ganson and Kate the maid soon got to work with strips of paper and glue to try to seal it off.

The station at Steyning was about a mile from our house. It was on a branch of the Brighton Line and had a goods yard. Cyril and I often went there to watch the little tank engine sorting out the trucks. She was painted mustard yellow with L.B. & S.C.R. on her side and a bright copper band round the top of her funnel. I was beginning to take a great interest in engines, and could classify them – 2-4-0, 4-4-2, and so on – according to the arrangement of their wheels. One day we saw a real tender engine standing in a siding, a 2-4-2 passenger locomotive. We climbed the fence and had a good look at her. The fireman was polishing her with an oily rag and we sidled close up to him. He turned and said, 'Fond of engines, eh?' 'Oh yes!' I replied. Then boldly I asked: 'Could we please have a look in the cab?' The fireman called: 'Tom, 'ere's a couple wants to look in your cab.' A head peered over the side, then a voice said: 'Come up, but mind the oil!' Cyril and I scrambled up, not minding the oil, and there we were on the footplate of a real engine. Tom then explained what all the taps and handles and gauges meant and how the reversing gear worked. Everything was polished and shining and he was rightly proud of his engine. 'How does she start?' I asked breathlessly. 'Hold tight and I'll show you,' Tom answered. 'Stand clear, Dave!' and he pulled a handle. We moved steadily forward to the stop block, stopped, and reversed. One of my life's ambitions had been achieved and I could hardly find voice to thank him. 'That's all right, son,' he said. 'Perhaps you'll drive an engine yourself one day.' Aunt Ellen was rather horrified when she heard of our exploit, but reassured when we told her we had not travelled far.

We were sorry when the time came for us to leave, but as we said goodbye our aunt said she would ask us again. 'If I'm spared!' she added. We were able to visit her almost every year, and long after I was married my wife and I often took the children to stay at her house. She never got over her abhorrence of tobacco, so when I wanted to smoke I had to take my pipe into the garden. She would watch me from the sitting-room window, smiling and shaking her head, rather as if I were a naughty schoolboy.

There were a few days to go before the end of the holidays and I spent them trying to catch up on my holiday task.

Lizzie had told us on our return that she had seen a paragraph in the paper saying that Frank Dicksee had been injured. It seemed that he had stopped a runaway horse. 'A brave act,' the paper said. We promptly went to Fitzroy Square to inquire after him, and found him in bed with a large cage covering his legs. His sister told us that he had arrived home in a cab with torn trousers and a battered top hat, and it was not until he had undressed that he realized the state of his leg, which had a wound from knee to ankle. The doctor, after dressing it, packed him off to bed, and there he had to stay for a fortnight. Frank told us it was a carriage and pair that caused the trouble. The horses took fright and bolted. He caught the flying reins but was knocked down and kicked. He was very modest about it all and joked about the colour of his other leg, which he said was pea green. He told us he had bought a house in St John's Wood, and that as soon as the necessary alterations had been made he and his two sisters and their aunt, Miss Alice Bernard, would be moving. The house, in Greville Place, was a late Regency building with a pleasant garden. A studio was to be built at the back, and Frank would then give up the studio in Peel Street.

After they had moved, and before the studio was finished, we often went to see them on Sunday. Their niece, little Ethel Dicksee, was sometimes there and it was fun playing in the new building. Little Ethel and her Aunt Dolly Burroughes, who was only two years her senior, Cyril and I would clamber and chase about and get our clothes in a nice mess.

Among the musicians we met at the Dicksees' was a **Dr Armbruster**. Besides being a conductor, he was a very good pianist. He was also a great Baconian, and he told us that he had proved that Bacon wrote all Shakespeare's plays. He then proceeded to claim that Bacon was a German. With Teutonic thoroughness he had marshalled his 'facts' and it was useless to argue with him.

Father was rather concerned about the work that Lizzie had to do, and he consulted Polly Dicksee about it. She promised to find a girl to help with the housework. Soon she wrote to say that she had heard of a young relative of their cook whom she thought would be suitable. The girl, who had only just left school and was very small and shy, came with her mother, and it was all arranged. Her name was Virtuella. She was very willing, and Lizzie, though not without misgivings, said she would 'do'. Though Virtuella did her best she was not adept at answering the door. On the principle that all visitors must be made welcome, the gas man was shown into the drawing-room. It was pointed out that some discrimination should be exercised with strangers. We had finished supper one night and were sitting in the drawing-room when there was a knock at the door and an agitated Virtuella put her head into the room and quavered, 'Please, sir! There's a rough man outside!' Father went down to investigate and found the front door on the chain. He opened it cautiously. Outside was a figure in a wideawake hat and heavy cape. It was Mr Stacpoole, the artist from next door, come to call.

Chapter Six

ST PAUL'S

I RARELY saw my uncle at school as his classroom was among the high-ups on the top floor. Occasionally I caught sight of him descending the stairs in his mortar-board and gown, or passing to the Masters' Common Room. He was very near-sighted and I never did anything to attract his attention, except once when Father had given me a note to deliver to him and I tried to catch him during Break. He was deep in conversation with another master, and I had to wait until after school hours, when I boldly braved the sanctity of the top corridor and waylaid him as he left his classroom. He looked surprised at being accosted by a small boy and peered at me curiously through his glasses.

'Please, sir,' I stammered, 'I have a letter for you from my father.'

'Oh!' he said. 'Your father, eh!' It was clear he did not recognize me.

I handed him the note. He removed his glasses and put on another pair. Then I said, 'Please, sir, I am your nephew Ernest.'

A smile lit up his face. 'Dear me! Why yes, of course, of course. How stupid of me not to recognize you, but I am near-

sighted, you know. Well, and how do you like being at St Paul's?'

'I like it very much, thank you, Uncle Willie,' I replied.

He stood smiling at me and then said: 'Oh yes, the note! Let us see what your father has to say.' Having read the letter he asked: 'And how do you like your new home?'

'Very much thank you, sir – Uncle Willie.'

'Well, tell your father I will write to him.'

'Thank you, s – Uncle Willie.' And I bolted.

It was different with the High Master – the 'Old Man' as we called him. We saw him all too often. The worst punishment that could be inflicted upon any boy was to be sent from the classroom to wait outside until recalled. The Old Man had a habit of going the rounds and descending on a classroom without warning. He would sail majestically down the corridor, and it was useless for any boy doing penance outside a door to try and hide behind the lockers. He was spotted from afar and the enemy bore down on him. With a growl he was asked what he was doing there. A stammering explanation was sure to be cut short with 'Speak up'. Then, 'What's your name?' The door was flung open and he was sent to his place. I think most of the masters dreaded these visitations as much as we did. If the Old Man was heard approaching it was the signal for all to assume an air of intense industry and lamb-like innocence. Each junior master was provided with a cane, though I do not think the weapons were often used. Only once was I caned, and I have no doubt that I had earned the punishment. It was dealt out by Mr Wainwright, and Broad suffered at the same time. It was not laid on heavily, but my behind was tender for days. The worst crimes were 'tried' by the High Master, and if the deed were proved it meant a 'portering', a chastisement administered by the head porter, a great bearded fellow. Rumour said that this really hurt.

Wainwright's formroom was on the top floor, with a fine view over south London towards Earls Court. We could see the Exhibition buildings going up and the Great Wheel in the process of construction. My desk was luckily placed near the window, and I could watch the structure gradually rising above the surrounding buildings. First the supporting arms: then the great round hub, 150 feet above ground-level: then the steel spokes. When finished it looked very much like a gigantic bicycle wheel with railway carriages hung round the tyre. But the wheel was not a great success; it stuck on several occasions and unfortunate passengers were marooned for hours in the sky. One advantage of being in 'Wainwright's' was that the Old Man rarely penetrated as far as our corridor on the top floor. It was the abode of the science forms and included the laboratory.

Broad and I were moved to 'Chater's' after two terms, with a class-room on the ground floor, where we were never safe from surprise visitations. On the whole, however, we liked 'Chater's', though our form master was apt to be sarcastic, a trait hated by schoolboys. We learnt history and English and did readings from *Twelfth Night*. So far I had done no science; that was to come later when I was moved up to Thomas's form, where the work was really interesting, for we were given periods of practical science and physiology and it became the fashion to write long essays on these subjects for homework. We vied with each other to produce the longest essay. Thomas would look over the closely written foolscap sheets, tugging at his moustache, then throw them on his desk saying, 'It may amuse you, but it bores me – take the rotten stuff away.' For physiology we went to Dr Watt's classroom. We liked him. He was a thin, active little man, and he really taught me a lot. As there was another master named Holmes it was only natural for us to couple them together – Trevelyan Holmes and his friend Dr Watts is how we referred to them, and it was rumoured they went crime-hunting together. One day a week we listened to Watkins talking on physics. He pumped air out of bottles to create vacua and drew diagrams on the black-board. We were supposed to take notes, but mine were very sketchy. Part of our time was spent in the laboratory. We were nominally in charge of Mr Wright, known as 'Bottlewasher'. He had no sense of authority and we practically did as we liked, spending much time in unauthorized and risky experiments. Lined up at the benches with a bunsen burner and blower, we would try to produce a coloured bead from certain white powders, or start dissolving things in nitric acid. Once there was a loud explosion, which sent Bottlewasher rushing to the corner where a boy had burnt his hands badly. The sulphuretted hydrogen was kept in a glass cupboard, and whenever we had occasion to go there we made a point of leaving the door open so that the smell gradually spread across the laboratory until it reached Bottlewasher. We would all start coughing and making as much fuss as possible while he hurried to the cupboard and threatened to report us all. We would quench our thirst by concocting lemonade. We made it from bicarbonate of soda, citric and tartaric acids. I do not think it can have been good for us, for we had no idea of the right proportions, but it fizzed and was quite refreshing.

Two mornings a week we worked in the drawing school. This was a great change from Bewsher's. It was well provided with casts from the antique and the walls were hung with drawings by Old Paulines. Among these was one by Everard Calthrop, a charcoal study of Hammersmith Bridge. What pleased me most was the encouragement I was given to put my own visual thoughts on paper. I drew every sort of subject, with a preference for battle scenes, and I usually produced one or two by way of homework. The art school was the place where the great and the small came in contact. It was there that I saw G. K. Chesterton and Compton Mackenzie (he was 'Compton' then).

We were taught by Mr Harris. He would often cry: 'If yer do it again I'll cane yer,' but I never knew him do so. Then there were the two assistant masters, 'Foxy' Holden and his younger brother

A preference for battle scenes. Age 14

'Baby'. They seemed to be able to tackle any form of art, including theoretical perspective, which I never succeeded in mastering.

I was soon promoted to a drawing-board and a stool to make studies from the antique. There were one or two lucky fellows who spent most of their time in the art school, and later on, in my last two terms, I was to join them in what was called 'the Special Drawing Class'.

The High Master had raised the standard of work in the school so much that St Paul's had won the highest number of scholarships at the universities of any of the public schools. The Old Man was a keen scholarship-hunter, and when he learned that I was going to make Art my profession, he made it clear to me that I was expected to secure a scholarship to the Royal Academy Schools. He became quite affable to me when he visited the Art School. Indeed, it was almost embarrassing to have a heavy hand laid on my shoulder and to hear a gruff voice saying: 'And how is our young artist getting on?'

Working in the Art Class I got to know two older boys who were, I think, in the Army Class, Ritchie and Collison Morley. Collison Morley was as keen on soldiering as I was and he showed me drawings he had made while following the army manœuvres the previous autumn. On leaving school he joined the Territorials and rose to command a London battalion. He was killed at the battle of Loos in September 1915. Ritchie passed into the Regular Army and was given a commission in the Scottish Rifles. At the battle of Givenchy in the spring of 1915 the Scottish Rifles were cut to pieces, losing most of their officers. Ritchie and Watkiss Lloyd, who was a friend of my early childhood in Kent Terrace, were both killed. How glad they would have been to know that, fifty years later, plans for the greatest military operation of all time were to be made by an Old Pauline in this same building.

The winter I was moved from Bewsher's to St Paul's was a memorable one for the big school, which that year had one of the finest rugger sides in its history. In the team were Clementi Smith, Bailey, 'Milky' Stedman and Ricketts, the last a brilliant full back who helped to win all their matches save one – either Tonbridge or Bedford. How we stood behind the ropes and cheered 'P-A-U-L-S'! It could be heard all down the Hammersmith Road, fathers, mothers and sisters joining in. I enjoyed playing rugger in 'Little Side'. Being small and quick I played at half-back. Cyril was big enough to be a forward and was put on Middle Side. He did well enough to be moved up to Big Side and then got his third fifteen colours. He left school at seventeen so he had no chance of rising higher.

At cricket at that time the school shone less brightly. But in athletics there were two good runners in Francis Williams and

St Clair Smith, both of whom broke school records, Williams for the mile and 'Tommy' Smith the hundred yards. Lacrosse was played in the Easter term, but I do not think it was very popular: it was almost impossible to get match fixtures, for no other schools played the game, and though there were a few club opponents they were far away and in any case greatly outclassed the school.

Then of course there was the Cadet Corps. In spite of my keenness on soldiering I could not summon up enough enthusiasm to ask Father if I could join it. It was not exciting to parade on the gravel at the back, slope arms and form fours, march and counter-march, in recreation time. In any case I was too small to join the ranks. This was before the days of properly organized camps when all the schools went to Salisbury Plain at the beginning of the summer holidays and were given regular field days and sham fights.

The year after I started at St Paul's the Aunts took their summer holidays at Shalford, near Guildford. They rented the Vicarage and, in accordance with the now-established custom (which continued for three more years), we were invited to stay with them. We had a grand holiday. Our cousins from Kensington had taken a house on Guildown which could be reached easily by ferry across the river at St Catherine's, and we were always in and out of one another's houses. The cousins were a large family, five girls and two boys. Douglas, the youngest, was several years our junior, but a most sporting boy and a great acrobat. He distinguished himself later by entering the Café Royal walking on his hands with his feet in the air.

We had picnic parties together, and were fond of sitting on the railway bank between the two tunnels by St Catherine's and watching the trains steam by. The grown-ups had solemn croquet parties on the Vicarage lawn. To one of these the local curate and his wife were invited. During the game Aunt Emily made one mighty swipe

76

and we watched, horrified, as the ball bounded across the lawn straight for the legs of the curate, who was deep in conversation with his back turned to the game. The ball caught him fair and square, and with a loud squawk he leapt in the air. Poor Aunt Emily was never allowed to forget this sad affair.

The Vicarage garden ran alongside the main road and had a stream at the bottom. On the other side of this was a potting-shed and the tool-house. Cyril and I soon discovered that the gardener kept an old tricycle in the shed and that the door was unlocked. The man only worked three days a week, so on his off days we would trundle the machine out and ride it round the garden. We pushed it up the slope and then had a fine down-hill run to the stream. Alas! the brakes were not to be relied on and the inevitable happened.

We were both on the machine when it got out of hand and we landed in the stream. We did our best to clean it up, but it still bore traces of mud when the gardener came again, and we were severely reprimanded. The shed was henceforth locked, and that was the end of that little game.

During our stay at Shalford we took some picnics on the river. Boats could be hired at The Jolly Farmer, and though we were not supposed to go on the water without a grown-up in charge, we managed occasionally to get a punt and go off on our own. I expect the man in charge of the boats knew that it was almost impossible to upset a punt.

It was the best summer holiday we had had for years and I was sorry when September came and we had to go back to school. Father must have been better off at this time, for we were allowed more pocket-money, and Cyril and I made the most of it. We would save up and then have an evening at the Lyric Opera House. I do not know why it was called 'Opera House', for I never heard of an opera being performed there. It was not until Nigel Playfair took it over and produced *The Beggar's Opera* that this happened; then it was renamed 'The Lyric Theatre'. In the nineties it was the home of melodrama. There were frequent changes of programme and a seat in the pit could be had for ninepence. We would scan the posters and lay out our limited funds on something really spicy,

Secured some luggage and made for a barn

such as *East Lynne* or *The Still Alarm*. The latter involved the presence of a real steam fire-engine at work on the stage. We also saw a drama about an innocent man wrongly convicted. His escape from Dartmoor in broad-arrow clothes, with the old lag (comic relief) and a young boy, was sensational. The boy was played by a buxom girl with a fair wig. How one of such tender years came to be 'doing time' in the prison was difficult to understand. Anyway, they escaped and, profiting by a most realistic railway accident, for which the villain was responsible, they secured some luggage and made for a barn. Climbing up the ladder to the hayloft was too much for the 'boy's' breeches; they split at the back and the curtain came down amid tumultuous applause.

Almost our favourite was *For the Honour of the House*. This was high melodrama if you like! The villain, hissed by the whole house whenever he appeared, was foiled in the end, though it was a near thing. He had lured the heroine to a lonely part of the Alps and left her there, bound and helpless, to die in the stage snow. The audience waited, tensely anxious. Would the hero arrive in time? Distant shouts were heard! The heroine raised her voice in a despairing cry, and on to the stage lumbered a full-grown St Bernard dog, plough-

ing his way through the 'snow'. This, of course, brought down the house, and I doubt if there was a dry eye among the audience.

Lower down King Street was another playhouse, the Hammersmith Palace of Varieties. 'The Temple', as it was called, produced shows of a not very high standard but perfectly respectable and usually rather dull. A seat in the gallery cost fourpence, and one sat in extreme discomfort with the knees pressed against the back of the seat in front. The floor of the auditorium sloped very steeply and gave the feeling that a false step would mean landing in the pit. Any unpopular turn was continually interrupted by loud comments from the audience.

We did not tell Father that we went there, for we knew that he had a prejudice against music-halls. I don't think he had ever been to one himself; he regarded all music-halls as haunts of vice. No doubt this was due to his upbringing, for my grandfather's views on all things theatrical, even the legitimate drama, were extreme, and my aunts were never allowed to go to a theatre. I know Father often went to the theatre with his friends, and after his engagement he used to take Mother, who had many friends in the profession, among them Ellen Terry.

Additional pocket-money enabled Cyril and me to break out in other ways than the theatre. We tried smoking. 'Woodbines' were five a penny, and we would indulge in a packet and smoke them on the sly, either in the summer-house in Broad's garden or, if we knew Father would be out for the evening, in our own bedroom at home. One afternoon Broad and I bought a packet of Woodbines after school. Crossing Hammersmith Bridge and turning down to the tow-path we found a dark corner and lit up. It was quite secluded under the bridge, so we thought we were safe and were pulling away when to our horror we saw Wainwright approaching. We had taken the precaution of hiding our school caps in our pockets. We dived behind a pier and cowered there while he passed quite close to us. I do not think he even noticed us, but for days I was in terror, expecting to be hauled up before the 'Old Man'.

Chapter Seven

TO BE AN ARTIST

IT was during my last year at St Paul's that I began to take a real interest in music. Ethel, by now an accomplished pianist, would play Bach to me by the hour. I did not understand it, and the variations seemed, to my uninformed mind, monotonous. I would complain: 'But, Ethel, there are no tunes.' She would painstakingly try to explain how fugues did not depend on tunes, but it was many years before I understood what she meant, and I was always relieved when she turned to Chopin. Ethel had an excellent musical memory, besides being able to read music at sight, and when asked to play at the Dicksees' or at other friends' homes would sit down and play without music.

I had one friend at the school who was keen on music. His name was Peyton; we called him Pen. I sometimes went to his home in Holland Road and listened to him playing the piano. He told me that his family had a young friend with a beautiful singing voice, and he invited me to come and hear her sing one evening. I was astonished to find she possessed a long fair pigtail. Her name was Muriel George, and she can only have been about fifteen years old, but her voice was mature and perfectly trained. She sang to us all the evening. I had never heard anything like it and was quite overcome. She told us that she was going to make singing her profession. After school broke up in July the Peytons took a house at Dachet, and asked Cyril and me to spend the day with them. Muriel was

there, and after an early supper we all went on the river. While we drifted slowly along she sang to us. Passing boats stopped, and people came out of house-boats to listen, and though I have often heard her voice since then it is that evening that stays in my memory.

By now I had quite definitely settled that I would be an

artist. This pleased Father and he gave me every encouragement. 'Heatherley's' was chosen from among the many art schools, because Father had once attended evening classes there. I was, of course, eager to start, but I was only fifteen, and was told that I must have at least another year at St Paul's. I did not consider what effect

Drawn for my homework, age 15

leaving school so early would have on my general education, and I have often thought that another two years would have given me a better start in life. However, there it was; I was earmarked by the High Master for a scholarship and was put into the 'Special Drawing Class'. Needless to say, I enjoyed it, and in spite of my fondness for music, violin-playing ceased to interest me.

85

As the only member of the Special Drawing Class I had a very independent time. I could choose the particular cast I wanted to draw. Homework was no longer labour, for I was always drawing at home, anyway, and therefore had plenty of sketches to show each day. Nominally in Thomas's form I had only to do French or Mathematics twice a week.

That summer term Cyril left St Paul's. It was sad for him, as it meant that he would have to work in an office in the City, and, instead of five weeks in the summer, with Christmas and Easter as well, his holidays would be limited to a fortnight. He went as clerk to a firm of underwriters at Lloyd's. However, this had the compensation of placing him in the proud position of earning a salary and of being a 'City Gent', on the strength of which he bought himself a bowler hat.

I spent my holiday with the Aunts. They had taken a house at Eastbourne, a girls' school, in Selwyn Road. There were far too many bedrooms and most of the top floor was shut up. The greatest asset of the building, in my opinion, was a fully equipped gymnasium where I spent hours climbing ropes and swinging on rings. There was companionship in the person of a young man called Charlie,

who came every day to chop wood or carry coals and to attend to the fat, round and docile pony which was needed to pull the chaise. Once it had been established that the pony was quiet and the chaise safe, Aunt Alicia ventured out in it, Charlie driving her round the links. Even the invalid Aunt Annie was persuaded to embark. The chaise was the shape of a huge Bath chair on four wheels and so close to the ground it could not possibly turn over. It was very much the same as the one Queen Victoria is pictured as driving in the grounds of Balmoral.

In the gymnasium Charlie gave me lessons in climbing, and before long I could get to the top of the rope and slap the rafter. It was much more difficult to climb the pole, and it was some weeks before I accomplished it.

There was a large garden with a tennis court, but it was not well kept and we hardly played at all; in fact, it was not until Cyril arrived for his two weeks' holiday that I made great efforts to cut the grass properly, and to mark it out. Cyril came down one Saturday evening and said he was very lucky to get his holiday in August; it had only been possible because one of the other clerks had switched his holiday at the last minute.

With the tennis court and the gymnasium we had plenty to amuse us, and we also took long walks over the Downs. Sometimes Father and Ethel would accompany us, and we would all go off for the day, getting a sandwich or bread-and-cheese lunch at a public house (Ethel and I had to sit outside). We walked for miles, to Birling Gap, Friston, East Dean and then to Alfriston. Father always made a bee-line for a church and generally found something interesting. His great find was at Alfriston. While we were looking round the church he was exploring a jungle of weeds and bushes close by where there was a tumbledown building. We heard him call out:

'I say, boys, I've found something.' We joined him at once. He was almost dancing with excitement. 'I believe this is an old clergy house,' he said, and dived in through the broken doorway. 'Yes, look! There are the rafters of the roof, and this is a little chamber alongside.' The floor was roughly paved, but matted with weeds. The walls were of stone and fairly sound, but the roof was half gone and the whole place covered with bird-droppings. We spent a long time there while Father paced it out and made notes in his pocket-book. Outside, the weeds and shrubs were so thick we could hardly get through, and in some places they had grown into the walls. It was late before Father could tear himself away. 'I wonder,' he said, 'if the Vicar knows what this really is. It is unique, quite unique!' When we reached home Father wrote a letter to the authorities and, I have no doubt, to the Vicar as well, telling them what he considered should be done to save the building. It is now, of course, well known and, having been restored, is one of the ecclesiastical gems of Sussex.

It seemed a very short fortnight for Cyril, but we found time to go down to the front and listen to 'Dan Randall' and his troupe. Dan was a long way behind the great Harry Randall of the 'Halls', but he made us laugh. It was not a good summer for bathing; too

many cold winds and boisterous seas. One morning Charlie came with the news that a vessel had been driven ashore and was lying on the beach. We were off in no time, and found a crowd gathered to watch a coasting ketch being smashed to pieces in the breakers. The crew of three had struggled ashore; a narrow escape for them, for the mast had come down and the vessel had broken her back. She carried a cargo of cement and the bags were stacked inside, setting in the wet, with the ship's timbers falling away. I had never seen a shipwreck before, and it struck me as a very melancholy sight. A bystander told me that the ship had sprung a leak off Beachy Head and the skipper realized their only chance was to run her ashore.

In Selwyn Road there was a house that stood below ours: it had a garden separated from us by a low brick wall, and one day, to my surprise, I saw a fellow Pauline in the garden. He was a foreigner named Camacho and he told me that his father was the Brazilian Consul in London. They had taken the house for the summer. He went to fetch his sisters and we all talked over the garden wall. The sisters were most attractive little girls with long black pigtails, and

89

we would often meet by the garden wall. They told us they would be having a garden party soon and that if we looked over the wall we would see it all. When the day came Cyril and I watched all the preparations: a marquee was erected, coloured flags hung up, and when the guests came we had a grandstand view of the proceedings. There was a band playing, and presently the girls came running up in smart white frocks to ask us if we would like some ices. Needless to say we said 'Yes, please,' whereupon they darted off and came back with a tray full of ices into which we all tucked away until the girls were called. 'Now we have to dance,' they told us; 'but wait here and we'll be back.' We watched the dance: a group of little girls prancing around. Then they came flying back with more ices.

On Cyril's last morning we got up early and tried to play a last game of tennis, but the dew on the grass made the balls too wet. As a result we had to run nearly all the way to the station. After his departure I missed him terribly. The Aunts did not seem to understand that we needed companionship of our own age.

A few days later there was a terrific thunderstorm at night. I was lying awake in bed watching the lightning when an agitated Aunt Emily appeared. She was collecting the fire-irons from each room and putting them under the beds. It appeared some friend had told her that fire-irons attracted the lightning down the chimney. When she had gone I crept out of bed and went to Ethel's room. She too had had a visit from Aunt Emily, and we had a good laugh about it all.

The winter that year was long and bitterly cold, with the usual accompaniment of burst pipes. We went skating in Richmond Park, and both the Serpentine and the Long Water in Kensington Gardens were frozen over and safe enough to bear crowds of skaters. After Christmas, with the Pantomime season in full swing, Cyril and I

saved up our pocket-money and went to the half-crown pit at Drury
Lane. It was not my first visit to the Lane, for I had been to
Pantomime before, and on one unforgettable occasion spent the
evening in a box. This time it was the pit with a two-hour wait
outside the heavy double doors, which looked like the entrance to
a prison. Itinerant musicians helped to pass the time. When the
opening time arrived, muffled footsteps sounded within, then the
rattle of bolts being withdrawn – and the crowd did the rest. There
was a stampede, the opener running as if for his life. Once inside,
the young and agile, able to jump over the back seats and seize
places in the front row, scored heavily. It was a happy sensation to
settle down in the hard-won seat and watch the house light up, the
audience arrive and the orchestra file in, all too slowly. Finally, to
a round of applause, Dan Godfrey took his place on the conductor's
stand. All this for a carefully hoarded half-crown. I cannot remember
what the pantomime was about but I know we had Dan Leno and
Herbert Campbell – an immortal combination – Fred Emney the
Elder, with Laurie and Zanfretta. Nor do I know who played the
principal boy, though I am sure she was quite as ravishing as the
'Boy' I had seen seven years before. I did not suffer the pangs of
unrequited love on this occasion; surely a warning sign of advancing
age. I was beginning to grow up and I knew that I was about to
enter on my last term at St Paul's.

Chapter Eight

HEATHERLEY'S

ALTHOUGH technically still a schoolboy I felt I had one foot in the great world when Father arranged for me to spend Saturdays working at Heatherley's. I felt very small, as indeed I was at sixteen, when I took my place in the Art Class among the free and easy students, some of them grown men with beards, to draw from the living model. I found drawing from life very different from the casts I had been used to.

The principal of Heatherley's was John Crompton, an imposing presence. He wore a beige frock-coat and a flowing salmon-pink tie. He was a small man, but his carriage lent him height so that he seemed to tower above me. To be addressed as Mister Shepard was startling. His criticisms were conducted in the plural. Standing before my drawing he would say: 'If we look at our legs, Mister Shepard, I think we shall find them a trifle on the heavy side.' Nothing seemed to put him out and he never forgot his dignity. It was a rare thing to see him smile.

Heatherley's had an interesting history. It had been established for many years and was the original of Thackeray's 'Gandishes' in the *Newcomes*. It certainly preserved its old-world atmosphere. The house in Newman Street had been converted to serve the purpose of an art school. Passing through the house one descended three steps to the Antique School, crowded with plaster statues. Beyond this was the Costume Studio, with benches and 'donkeys' disposed

Never forgot his dignity

round the model's throne. A large choice of costumes was available, and these were sometimes arranged to suit the convenience of what might be called the permanent students. I hesitate to use the word 'student' for elderly ladies, but I feel the atmosphere at Heatherley's at that time was regulated by their presence. Many would-be Academy pictures were painted within its sacred walls, when cavaliers and pirates were the vogue for subject pictures.

With so much to look forward to, my last term at St Paul's was quite a pleasant one. In July, Father told me that the Aunts were renting a house in Hampshire for the summer. This pleased me immensely, for if we stayed with them, as we usually did, I should have the chance to see the army at work. So it happened. After school broke up we received the expected invitation, and in due time Ethel and I found ourselves in the train for Bentley, near Farnham.

Aunt Fanny met us, wearing a shady straw hat and, with her skirts girded up, looking very summery. A pleasant walk across fields brought us to the 'Welches'. The house, attractive and roomy, looks much the same today. It had large grounds, a paddock, a tennis court, and a fine kitchen garden surrounded by an old red-brick wall. On this wall were peach, nectarine and plum trees, a delectable sight. There were stables and outhouses at the back, where a man was grooming a very fine horse which he said was a thoroughbred.  We had a warm welcome from the Aunts, and from the maids as well. It was the first time that I had stayed in such a mansion, and I very much enjoyed the novelty, especially as having the run of such a well-stocked garden meant a lot to a boy of my age.

On making inquiries about the military I was told by Mary the maid that there were a lot of soldiers about. I was glad when Father arrived from London on his bicycle the next day, for I was itching to borrow it and set off on the Aldershot road. The next morning I was up early, and walking towards Farnham I came on some engineers with a wagon fixing up wires on a pole. Then some helmeted cavalry trotted by. 'Dragoons,' I thought. Things were warming up. I ran home and swallowed some breakfast, then borrowed Father's cycle and set off. I had no difficulty in picking up the trail of the troops, for the roadside was littered with empty 'Woodbine' packets. Presently I overtook the tail end of the column –

camp cookers and ration carts. It was getting very hot, and the cooks had unbuttoned their tunics and some had dock leaves stuck under their helmets. Farther along I came upon a lot of infantry halted by the roadside, and sheltering from the sun under the hedges; marching in the heat of the day in red tunics with helmets and pipeclayed belts can have been no fun. By now I was feeling like a real war correspondent and went ahead in search of adventure. I came upon it at a cross-roads, where an infantry outpost was disputing the advance of a cavalry patrol. The Hussars in full uniform dismounted and, creeping up, started taking pot-shots with their carbines at the redcoats. It was a mild form of warfare, and presently both sides settled down to an exchange of highly coloured badinage. I left them to go in search of something to eat, and found a small pub where I had bread and cheese and ginger-beer. In the afternoon I was in luck, for I saw a full-scale battle with a horse-drawn maxim gun chattering away and kilted and trousered infantry storming up-hill in close order, in the Inkerman style. I got into trouble when I reached home at nearly dinner-time, for I had caused grave anxiety among the Aunts by being out all day.

Father and I spent several days at Odiham, walking over there and carrying our sketching materials. It was my first experience of painting out of doors and my efforts were not a success. We had a festive time at Bentley, where we made several friends and were asked out to tennis parties. There was also a cricket match at which I distinguished myself by bowling our opponents' star batsman. I must confess that the condition of the pitch favoured me; whether the ball broke either way had nothing to do with my delivery. Cyril came down for his fortnight's holiday towards the end of our stay. He and I got up very early one cold and misty morning and went cubbing. The arrival of the hop-pickers in the neighbourhood

gave the gardener and his boy plenty to worry about, though their vigilance was rewarded and only a few apples were lost. It was mid-September when we went home.

When I began regular work at Heatherley's most of my time was taken up with drawing from the antique. I was not encouraged to do any painting, and never learned anything of construction or design. The tuition was not good and I often think I should have done better to have gone to the Slade where, under Tonks, more attention was

98

paid to good drawing and less to stippled finish. However, with the Scholarship to the Royal Academy Schools in view I had to stick to the prescribed course, and was much helped by seeing some drawings done the previous year by a student, George Stampa, who had been successful in winning the same scholarship for which I was trying. I looked at his drawings with awe and wondered if I could ever rise to such heights. George himself was, however, most reassuring.

I soon made friends with a boy of my own age, fresh from Haileybury, Arthur Connor. The son of a doctor, he lived with his parents at a house overlooking Clapham Junction Station. We had much in common and both of us felt strange in our new surroundings. I often went to tea at his home, where I met his sister Dot, a gay and charming schoolgirl of fourteen, and we all became great friends. I had acquired a nickname by this time, 'Kipper'. I think I earned it by somewhat gay and irresponsible behaviour, the expression 'Giddy Kipper' being a music-hall catch-phrase at that time. Anyway, it has stuck to me ever since, though usually shortened to 'Kip'.

It was later in the autumn when Chattie Wake appeared at Heatherley's. She came in one morning like a being from another world. With her copper-coloured hair she looked like a bacchante. Four or five of the younger students soon became a 'set' and livened the place up. Besides Chattie and Arthur Connor, there were Colyn Thompson, and Bartington, a young bearded American with a soft southern accent. We lunched together at 'Buck's' restaurant, next door to Heath's the hatters in Oxford Street. Our lunches were very frugal as we had little money. Arthur, who always had a good appetite, complained bitterly when funds were low. I managed better, for I soon found I could last all day on very little, knowing

that Lizzie would have a good meal ready for me when I arrived home in the evening. In the afternoon, when the old trouts had packed up work for the day, we played hockey amongst the casts in the antique school with a rolled-up paint rag for a ball, until the noise brought Crompton downstairs to register a dignified protest.

When I could borrow Father's bicycle I rode to work. I enjoyed this, for riding in the slow-moving traffic of those days had no terrors. I could cycle back with Chattie to her home in Cliveden Place, where she lived with her mother and sisters, wave goodbye to her there and pedal home to Hammersmith. Those happy months at Heatherley's were all too short. Our little 'Club' broke up early next year: Chattie to study at Rolshoven's in the Brompton Road, Colyn Thompson to study at the Slade, and 'Barty' to return to America. Had I not had to settle down to a hard grind on my Scholarship drawings, I should have missed them more even than I did.

Chapter Nine

DIAMOND JUBILEE

LONDON was full of exciting sights in the spring of 1897, the year of Queen Victoria's Diamond Jubilee. I borrowed Father's bicycle as often as I could so that, after work at Heatherley's, I could ride round the streets of the West End. Great stands were being erected in the streets, and in the parks camps were being made ready to receive troops from all parts of the Empire. London was very full; great numbers of people had come up from the provinces to see the preparations.

Soon after Easter Father was asked to play Malvolio in *Twelfth Night*, which was to be performed in the open air during the summer. The producer was Charles Fry. Malvolio was a part Father knew well, having played it several times with the Irving Club, an amateur dramatic society in which Henry Irving took a great interest and which had been the nursery of several distinguished actors. On one occasion Irving had lent the society the Lyceum Theatre for a production of *Henry IV*, and had been so impressed by Father's acting that he had offered him a place in his company. Father, however, knowing the hazards of an actor's life, wisely refused.

The outdoor performance of *Twelfth Night* was given in the grounds of a big house at Richmond, where there was a natural stage of smooth green turf with a fountain playing in front and a background of rhododendron bushes. It is strange, but no one gave a thought to the weather. There had been so many sunny days in June that no arrangements were made to provide for a break in the fine spell. Happily the day turned out blazingly hot, almost too hot for comfort in Elizabethan clothes and grease-paint. Cyril and I played minor roles and thoroughly enjoyed them. Indeed Cyril was bitten with a desire to go on the stage.

In spite of all the excitement I managed to get on with my drawing at Heatherley's. It was early in June when Chattie Wake asked me to a garden-party. She was living in rooms in Kensington, in a house overlooking one of the small squares, and the party took place in the square. I had the thrill of my young life when Chattie introduced me to Baden-Powell. He was then a Major, just back from Matabeleland. Dressed as he was in conventional frock-coat and top hat, his very bronzed features did not look at ease. Chattie introduced me with 'This young artist is very keen on soldiers'. I was quite tongue-tied, but Baden-Powell smiled broadly

and told me that he also was a bit of an artist. At length I plucked up the courage to ask him about Matabeleland. He said the great advantage of working with light horse was that one could be independent. Scouting over country day and night, camping rough and cooking when one could, was altogether a great life. One could learn a lot by keeping one's eyes open all the time. Spellbound, I said it must be wonderful. 'Yes,' he answered, 'it is a great game . . . a great game.' I cannot help wondering if he was not already thinking of his Boy Scouts.

The time for the Diamond Jubilee was now very near. Although I had seen something of Queen Victoria's Golden Jubilee in 1887 when I was a small boy and lived near Regent's Park, we children had not seen the procession itself. Now, this year, we were to join with our friends the Dicksees in hiring a room somewhere on the route. By answering an advertisement a room was found over a butcher's shop in the Westminster Bridge Road which the procession would pass on its tour of south London after the Thanksgiving Service in St Paul's Cathedral. Through the early summer the weather, though fine, had been cool, and the soldiers from Africa and the Indies must have found it trying in their canvas camps in the Park. The London populace, however, was in high spirits, and sure it would be 'Queen's Weather' on the day. They were right. June 22nd turned out to be one of the hottest days of the year.

We were up by five o'clock. Too excited to eat much breakfast, we waited for the carriage to come that was to drive us to our butcher's shop. The early morning was grey with a cool white mist, and we did not feel very hopeful about the weather. Our packets of sandwiches were in our hands and we were beginning to worry about the carriage when it turned up, with Frank, Pollie and Minnie inside. Father and Ethel joined them while Cyril and I scrambled up beside the driver. He was a gloomy man and not encouraging about the weather, which, he said, *might* clear later. We drove through Fulham and Putney to avoid the crowds north of the river. As we reached Lambeth people were already lining the kerbs. Many of them had spent the night on the pavements and were having a picnic breakfast. We had to make a detour to reach our shop, and it took our flyman some time to pick his way through the alleys so as to arrive at the back entrance. We could hear the noise in the street in front as we climbed the staircase to our third-floor room. The place smelled strongly of meat, but this diminished as we rose.

A continuous muffled roar came from the crowd below, with occasional bursts of cheering as detachments of soldiers marched up to line the streets. We could see everything that went on, for our room, being so high up, gave us a good view down the Westminster Bridge Road. There were loud cheers for the municipal sand-cart as it passed throwing grit on the roads. The horse, plodding slowly along, was decorated with rosettes on his harness and ribbons on his tail. Presently a band arrived and marched up and down the street. But by far the best entertainment came from the other side of the road, for our room was exactly opposite the old Canterbury Music Hall. All its windows were occupied by music-hall stars and we were given the latest songs, the crowds joining in the choruses. One of the favourites was:

She was a dear little dicky bird,
Cheep, cheep, cheep, she went.
Sweetly she sang to me
Till all my money was spent.
The last time we met,
We parted on fighting terms,
For she was one of the early birds,
And I was one of the worms.

It was my first introduction to community singing. Shouts of 'Give us another one, Gus!' or 'Come on, Charlie!' quite drowned the band. By this time the sun was blazing down and the St John Ambulance men were busy.

The Thanksgiving Service in St Paul's was timed for midday, and

presently the head of the procession came in sight. A strange hush
fell upon the crowds. First rode a solitary officer in the uniform of
the 2nd Life Guards, the tallest man in the British Army. It was so
quiet as he passed that the sound of his horse's hooves could be heard

clip, clop, but from the distance came a muffled roar of cheering telling us that the Queen's carriage was drawing near. The waves of sound grew gradually louder until the State carriage, drawn by eight cream-coloured horses with purple trappings, and moving at a steady walk, came in sight. It was an open carriage on 'C-springs' and it seemed to rock slightly though the pace was slow and stately. The little old lady, a bonnet with a white osprey feather on her head and a black-and-white parasol in her hand, kept bowing to left and right. She looked pale. We learned afterwards that she was overcome more by the warmth of her reception south of the river than by the heat of the day. Indeed she nearly broke down, the tears streaming down her face. There could be no doubt what she meant to her people.

The carriage was followed by a glittering array of Emperors, Kings and Princes, Grand Dukes and Heads of State in uniforms of all colours. I was particularly impressed by a magnificent old Hussar, and also by a Guard Cuirassier from Germany. The Indian Princes who followed were splendidly mounted and their turbans and swords shone with precious stones.

The procession of troops from overseas followed. It was headed by Lord Roberts on a white horse, a famous animal wearing a service medal on his harness. Marching in small detachments and led by British officers, the men had a great reception. Brown, black or white – red coats, blue coats, khaki – turbans, helmets, fezzes – they were all loudly cheered. The naval contingent pulling their nine-pounder guns and wearing their summer straw hats were given a special cheer, as were the guns of the Royal Horse Artillery.

It was all over before two o'clock. The Queen must have arrived back at Buckingham Palace and had her luncheon by that time and was no doubt being called on by the crowds outside to appear on the balcony in her wheeled chair. It was much later when we were able to leave our room and make our way home. The streets were thronged with people. Indeed, this was the case for the rest of the day and most of the night. We were very tired by the time we reached our own house. Lizzie had prepared us a high tea, which was very welcome, and as Cyril and I were determined to go out again and see the illuminations, Father insisted, most wisely, that we went upstairs to lie down. I know that I slept soundly, and it was dusk when I woke.

King Street was doing its best with fairy-lights and gas signs, but we wanted to see the shops and clubs in the West End. We fought our way to the top of a bus on Broadway and payed double fare for our seats, and then were stopped and told no farther when we reached Piccadilly. Everyone seemed to be in the same situation, and we joined the crowds moving along by Green Park. The only wheeled traffic we saw in the main streets were a couple of Royal Carriages trotting up St James's. These produced some desultory cheers. Piccadilly Circus was very gay. Small groups of revellers were dancing, coster girls with their lads, to the music of a concertina. Family parties were struggling to keep together in the crush by holding tightly to their children. All were gazing upwards at the illuminations.

Cyril and I progressed slowly up Regent Street, where the shops made a brave show, and when we reached Oxford Circus turned left down Oxford Street. It was a hot night, and jostling with the closely packed crowds after being up at such an early hour was beginning to tell on me. By the time we reached Marble Arch both of us had had enough. The decision to go home was right enough, but we had to discover a way of getting there. We found places on the kerb and sat down for a rest and to think things over. Quite a number of people seemed to be of the same mind, for the kerb

by the park was lined with tired family parties, the children fast asleep. Some of the small boys were making journeys to the drinking fountain near by and coming back with dripping handkerchiefs which were passed round and squeezed out. It was only with a great effort that we shook ourselves to life again; I was almost asleep when Cyril shouted in my ear. The thought of having to walk five miles or so back to Hammersmith was intolerable, but something had to be done. We decided to walk to Hyde Park Corner and try for a bus there. As we passed through the Park it seemed that many people were preparing to spend the night in the open.

We were lucky enough to find a bus, and, after a struggle, to board it. The journey to Hammersmith was very slow, for the bus was a 'pirate' and regulations about overloading did not seem to apply on Diamond Jubilee Day, nor regulations on fares. The conductor just charged everyone a shilling. In one case this nearly led to a free fight. King Street was still *en fête* as we crawled along it. When we reached home I was too tired to think of supper, and tumbled into bed as quickly as possible.

It was a few weeks later that a letter came from the Royal Academy telling me that I had been admitted on probation as a student, and that I was to attend with my drawing materials for a further examination to be held at the Schools. I think Father was as pleased as I was about this, for it meant that if I passed the further test, I should be given three years' free tuition. There were eight of us on probation, among them Cadogan Cowper, Gilbert Holiday and Fred Appleyard, and we worked together in the back school for a fortnight. I think we all passed the test. But I know that I gave a great sigh of relief when it was all over and I could look forward to a summer holiday before starting work at the Schools at the end of September.

On the evening of the first week of August Father came home in a state of great excitement. He had been spending the afternoon at 53 Gordon Square. Only two aunts, Alicia and Fanny, were living there now, for Aunt Emily, the youngest and the only stout one in the family, had passed away in the winter, and the invalid Aunt Annie had died the year before. Owing to these bereavements there was not to be the usual long summer holiday in a house rented in the country. My godmother knew we would be disappointed about this, so she suggested that Father should take us to France and they would help to pay our fares. When Father broke this news to us Cyril and I nearly stood on our heads with joy. To be going *abroad* seemed too good to be true. The first thing to do was to write letters of thanks, not such an irksome task as it had been three years before. Ethel made a special journey to Gordon Square to render her thanks in person.

Going abroad was a relatively simple undertaking in those days. No passports were required, and there were no currency regulations. An English golden sovereign was welcomed at any hotel or restaurant, and would fetch 25 francs or more. Cyril's holiday fell at the end of August, so our plans were made for then.

I cannot remember a greater thrill in my life than I felt on the morning we started off with our bags for Victoria Station on our first journey abroad. We travelled to Newhaven, and as the train passed the level-crossing in the town I saw the Channel boat lying alongside the quay. She had two funnels and was flying the French flag, but was not as big as I had expected.

Passing through the Customs took no time and we climbed aboard the S.S. *Tamise.* The ship was crowded and we piled our luggage in a corner where Ethel and Father found seats. Then Cyril and I started to look around. It was wonderful to be on board a real steamer and we explored her from stem to stern. When the time came for her to start there was very little fuss – a long blast on the hooter, the ropes were pulled in and we were off. It was a bright day with a fresh breeze, just how fresh we soon found when we left the shelter of Newhaven breakwater. *Tamise* began to pitch and to throw showers of spray over her bows. We ran in and out, dodging these, until stopped by a French sailor.

A great many people became sea-sick and the crew were kept busy handing round small basins. Some French nuns made particularly heavy weather of it. We went to see how Ethel and Father were getting on in their corner. Father looked rather green, but my sister was quite well and cheerfully joined us in going aft, where we got as near the stern as we could and enjoyed plunging up and down and seeing our wake fade away in the distance. About halfway across the Channel we passed the packet going to Newhaven and exchanged signals. She was a paddle-boat, steadier than we were, and not so crowded. Then some French fishing boats sailed by, waving to us and holding up fish as they passed. Then the coast of France appeared. I had once seen this through a telescope at Dover, but now, watching it grow larger and larger as we approached, was much more exciting. The sea calmed as we neared Dieppe and I was interested to see how quickly our sea-sick passengers revived; the nuns particularly became quite lively and vociferous.

The breakwater at the harbour entrance was lined with people waving to us. I suppose that the arrival of the daily packet was an event in the lives of many people. Everything looked so refreshingly different from England and the novelty of it all made a strong appeal to me. We moved very slowly up the harbour as if we were going right into the town, then the ship made a complete turn. There did not seem to be any room to spare, but she was handled skilfully and fetched up gently alongside the quay. The

gangways were run out and immediately a throng of French por-
ters rushed on board. We had to cling tightly to our bags, for
they almost fought for our luggage. Once ashore, we were herded
into a wooden shed where perspiring Customs men tried to cope
with the influx. '*Thé? Tabac? Alumettes?*' We had none of these and
were passed through.

I was particularly impressed by the French gendarmes, who
looked so picturesque after our London policemen. There was one
outside the gates, talking to a little man in a peaked cap with a brown
corduroy jacket and gaiters. Near him was a chaise with a speckled
white pony. Father said, 'Now I wonder if that can be Monsieur
Hotot? I had a letter to say that he would meet us.' The little man
came forward and handed Father a small card. 'Bonjour, M'sieu','
he said. Sure enough it was Monsieur Hotot. He introduced us to
the chaise and to a dog which appeared from underneath it. 'Fiaton,'
he said, indicating the dog with his whip. I did not know what he
meant by the word, but it turned out to be the dog's name. After
crowding our luggage on to the chaise we climbed the hill from
Dieppe, the pony straining upward while we walked beside. Our destination was Varengeville, about four miles away. Once on the level
we rattled along the *pavé*, with Fiaton running ahead. Father tried to
carry on a conversation with our host, but was not very successful.
Then Ethel, whose French was better, acted as interpreter. We pulled
up outside our *pension*, a small *estaminet* in the main village street.
Madame Hotot, several sizes larger than her husband, met us at the
door and showed us a front room with tables and a sanded floor that
did duty as a bar, and a smaller back room, separated from the bar
by a glass-topped door, which was to be our dining-room.

I was much intrigued by the display of bottles of all colours on
the shelves of the bar, also by the advertisements on the walls for

Rattled along the pavé

'BYRRH' and 'MAGGI'. Cyril and I were to share a small bedroom upstairs which looked over the main street to a butcher's shop labelled 'Boucherie, Charcuterie'. I was really very hungry, and when we had carried our traps upstairs I sat by the window, looking at the butcher's shop, waiting for tea. But time passed and nothing happened, so I consulted Father, who said they never had tea in

France. However, he spoke to Madame Hotot, who kindly produced some kind of sweet biscuit that helped to stay the pangs.

We had a happy five days at Varengeville. Father spent a lot of his time painting, carrying his camp-stool and white umbrella and settling down for the day, while we explored.

There was a yard at the back with chickens and ducks and a couple of geese. Here Monsieur Hotot spent most of his time, carrying in hay for the pony or working in the garden beyond. There were two tortoiseshell cats, lean and shy animals, who bolted when Cyril and I tried to make friends. Monsieur Hotot did not help in the bar: that was Madame's province. She spent the mornings, between her journeys to the kitchen, polishing the tables and glasses. Everything in the inn was spotlessly clean. She was a friendly soul and I tried to converse with her, but we did not get very far for my French was, and still is, rudimentary. She did her best to help me along by pointing to various articles and naming them, then making me repeat the word until I pronounced it correctly. She told me the way to the sea-shore, passing the church and the little cemetery and then down the steep wooded slope. The beach was not exciting – rocky and covered in seaweed.

In the evening the bar-parlour filled up with blue-bloused labourers. We watched them through our glass door while we had supper. When it grew dark a smoky little oil lamp was lighted, but by this time I was usually so sleepy I was glad to go to bed. It took me some time to get used to the French breakfast of coffee and rolls, and I was always ready for *déjeuner* at 12.30. Madame cooked this herself, though she had a young girl called Denise to help her.

The day we were to leave, Monsieur Hotot brought the chaise round from the yard and we gathered in the bar to say goodbye. Madame produced a bottle and filled six small glasses with brandy.

It was my first experience of a *petit verre* and I tried to swallow it too quickly, with the result that I choked. Solemnly we drank to 'La Belle France'. We drove to Dieppe station, Fiaton bounding ahead again. Waiting for the train to start I had a good look at the engine. It

did not impress me. It was black and dirty and had too many pipes and bits of extraneous machinery for my taste, and it hissed steam from every joint. The carriages were very narrow, with hard wooden seats, and the low platforms were quite different from ours at home and I thought inferior.

The journey was not a long one. When we reached Rouen we found a yellow bus in the yard labelled 'Hôtel de la Poste'. We climbed in along with several other people. The Hotel was an old-fashioned place with a yard in front adorned with plants in tubs. A gateway and iron railings separated this from the road. It had the air of an old coaching inn. It must since have been entirely rebuilt, for it is now quite a grand hotel.

Rouen, with its many lovely buildings, including the famous clock – a favourite subject with the water-colour painters of that period – still had the air of an old provincial town. The shops seemed never to close, and there was a pleasant bustling air about the place, also a distinctive and rather pleasant smell. The very horses had a different look from what I was used to. But what particularly pleased me was the number of soldiers about: little infantrymen in long dark-blue coats reaching below their knees and red trousers. Some very smart ones had white gaiters.

Cyril and I shared a room high up and at the back of our hotel. The window looked out over the roofs to the Cathedral, whose ornate iron spire showed above the houses. The Cathedral was surrounded by narrow streets of half-timbered houses, closely packed and leaning at all angles. How I wish now that I had made better use of my time by drawing some of these houses. They were very lovely; and they were completely destroyed in 1944, when all that part of the city was bombed and burnt and the Cathedral itself narrowly escaped destruction.

Besides spending hours in the Cathedral, we went up the road to St Ouen and on Sunday afternoon climbed the hill to Bon Secours. This was a regular Sunday promenade for the townsfolk. There were family parties, nursemaids with children, and more soldiers – little cavalrymen in light-blue tunics and red breeches carrying their sabres in the crooks of their arms. The weapons looked much too big for them.

One evening we spent an hour sitting outside a café near the big clock, and Father told us how, twenty-seven years before, he had sat in almost the same spot talking to an English friend. They were both

A regular Sunday promenade

students and were in Rouen together studying architecture when the crisis between France and Germany arose. It was July 1870, and the streets were thronged with people and soldiers shouting 'A Berlin'. Father's friend advised getting away as quickly as possible, and they were lucky enough to reach home before the storm broke.

Over a week had passed since we left home, and our holiday was more than half over, but we had one more treat in store. After four days in Rouen we took the train again and arrived in the late afternoon at Les Andelys. This time there was no bus waiting at the little station, but we found a porter with a barrow who took charge of our luggage and promised to deliver it to the 'Grand Cerf'. Father had been told of this inn by a fellow artist, who reckoned it to be one of the best examples of the period. This naturally caught Father's interest. The inn, a fine half-timbered building, was close to the church. In the hall was a circular panelled 'tambour' containing a

Hotel du Grand Cerf at Les Andelys

Drawn in Normandy, 1897

stairway. Viollet le Duc mentioned the Grand Cerf as being one of the outstanding examples of woodwork of the period of Francis I. I speak of it in the past tense, for it too shared the fate of the houses in Rouen. When in 1947 I went to Grand Andelys hoping to see the place again, nothing remained of the town but a heap of rubble. Only the church still stood.

We spent nearly a week there, for there was plenty to see. We walked the half-mile to the little town by the Seine called Petit Andelys, and from the towpath watched the long barges going upstream to Paris. We climbed the hill to the Château Gaillard, a grand ruined fort with a tragic history. Cyril and I explored the old stones, and in the little valley below the walls, pictured ourselves among the starving crowd of non-combatants who, turned out of the fortress, were denied passage by the invaders – 'Les Bouches Inutiles'.

In the evening we gathered for table d'hôte in the dining room. The company, largely composed of commercial travellers, was most entertaining; many of the jokes were at the expense of our waiting woman, who was quite equal to the situation and gave as good as she got. The local notary in particular was a great wit. He looked like Don Quixote in pince-nez and the exchange of repartee between

him and Marie provoked roars of laughter. I saw Father glancing rather nervously at Ethel, who understood French, on several occasions.

I was sad when our holiday came to an end and we had to leave the 'Grand Cerf'. On the last morning we drove to Gisors and had time to see something of the old town before catching the train to Dieppe. The night boat was lying alongside the quay and we put our luggage in charge of a porter while we had our evening meal in a restaurant facing the harbour. It was dark when we boarded the ship, which was an English paddle-boat named *Rouen*, more spacious than *Tamise* and certainly steadier. It was fine with a calm sea. Rather than spend a night in the stuffy cabin on hard narrow bunks, Cyril and I found a corner on deck. I made a pillow of my overcoat and lay on my back, watching the clouds drift across the moon, and reviewed all that had happened in the last few months. It had been a wonderful year for me, and I looked forward with enthusiasm to life as a student at the Royal Academy Schools.

Chapter Ten

THE ROYAL ACADEMY SCHOOLS

I KNEW that I should have a year's work in the Lower School before passing – I hoped! – into the Upper, and that, a certain standard having been reached, time would be allowed for painting from life and, in the case of male students, in attending life classes for drawing in the evenings. Men and women students did not work together in the painting schools and the women had no evening life class. We always understood the reason for this to be the objections of some of the more antiquated Royal Academicians, who considered that young lady students should never be called upon to behold the nude.

The Academy Schools possessed two curators, Herbert and Cauty. Cauty looked after us in the Lower School, and his slow and ponderous steps could be heard approaching down the corridor, warning us to get on with our work. Herbert, though somewhat more eccentric, was more popular.

The Keeper at that time was a man of Spanish origin named Calderon, a Royal Academician and an accomplished painter. He had a most aristocratic appearance. Given a ruff round his neck he would have made a perfect model for a Spanish Don.

We started work at ten o'clock and stopped at three. So long as my family lived at Hammersmith I usually cycled to the Schools, but early in the year we had been warned that Theresa Terrace was to be pulled down. It seemed that the whole property, a valuable one facing the main road, had been sold and that a row of shops was to be put up on the site. This distressed me greatly. I had grown fond of our home, and it was not likely we should find another house with a studio. Father, on the other hand, was not sorry to make a move. Hammersmith, he said, had never agreed with him. He suffered from rheumatism, and his doctor had ordered him to take a mineral water cure at a spa. Llandrindod Wells was suggested, and it was settled that we should all go there for our summer holiday.

I had never been in Wales, and was quite pleased at the prospect. For one thing I looked forward to trying my hand at landscape painting in oils. I intended to enter for an Academy Schools prize called the 'Creswick' of which the specified subject was 'A Bridge over a Trout

Herbert and Cauty, Curators at the Royal Academy Schools. Drawn in 1897

Stream', and Wales seemed just the place to find this. The size of the picture rather frightened me – about 4½ feet by 3; I did not see myself lugging a canvas of that size over the mountains. A fellow student put me up to having a folding canvas made, but while this reduced the size it increased the weight. When the time came for our holiday I was much concerned about the transport of my canvas and was not reassured when Father, Ethel and I arrived at Euston and saw the way it was being bundled into the van with all the other luggage.

Our destination was a private hotel called 'Ye Wells'. It had a most friendly atmosphere and stood facing a large stretch of common with hills beyond. The pump room where the waters were dispensed stood in the middle of the common, and every morning a procession of patients filed across to take their early libations of flat-iron water. Father joined them. I tasted the water once and found it most disagreeable.

The proprietress of our hotel, Mrs Smythe, had two daughters and a small son. With the younger daughter, Winnie, I soon struck up a friendship. She was sixteen, with a long, fair pigtail tied with a ribbon, and as tall as I was. When she could get away we stole out together for a walk on the common, which was more fun than playing parlour games with the other boarders.

For many days I was preoccupied with the hunt for a subject for my picture. There did not seem to be anything suitable in the immediate neighbourhood. One afternoon I joined in a picnic which involved driving several miles in a horse wagonette. This brought us to an old stone bridge over a tumbling stream. Just what I wanted! But the scene was much too far away for repeated visits, and I was obliged to recognize that I should have to do with something nearer at hand. In the end I settled for a cranky wooden bridge and a stream that was no more than a brook. Thereby I set myself a difficult task; but I really had no choice. Even this was two miles from our hotel, and lugging my canvas and traps to it was a tiring job. Fortunately I found a cottage near by where I could leave my picture from day to day. Very few people passed that way, and I was able to work undisturbed – except for the flies! They attacked me from

every side. At intervals I would leap to my feet and run round the rocks, but the flies would return directly I settled to work again.

I had one visitor. I spotted him crossing the wooden bridge but ignored his proximity. Presently I became aware of him standing close behind me.

A voice said ''Obby?'

'I beg your parden,' I said. 'I . . .'

''Obby?' said the voice more loudly.

'Oh yes, it is, in a sort of way.' I turned my head and saw a small man smoking a curly briar pipe. He came nearer and regarded my canvas.

'Flies a bit troublesome, I expect,' he said, as a cloud of them scattered at the smell of his tobacco. 'You want to smoke a pipe on a job like that.' Then, 'What are you painting?'

'I'm trying to paint the bridge.'

'Oh! That! Don't call that a bridge.' After a pause he went on. 'My old father was a bit of an artis' – took to painting after he retired.' He said this as if art were the drink. ' 'E didn't do big 'uns, but he did 'em quick, real shiny slap-up pictures, nice bright colours, gold framed an' all.'

I surveyed my own effort with loathing, and muttered acquiescence.

'Going to frame that one?'

'I can't say till it's finished.'

'Ah!' he said. 'Cost you a bit if you do.' And after a pause he said, 'You'd 'a' done better farther down. Much prettier and there's a stone bridge below the pool. Ah well, we all 'as our tastes. I must get along.' He left me to carry on my struggle with the despised bridge and the flies.

At length the time came when I could do no more. As I had to lug all my traps back to the hotel I chose a day when I knew the boarders would be out; I felt sure they would want to see my picture if they knew that I had brought it back. So I consulted Winnie, and we arranged that she should meet me at the back door and help me to hide it. We felt like two smugglers as we hid the picture in an empty room, where it remained till I went home ten days later. It was my first attempt at landscape painting in oils and I made the mistake of painting on the spot. Working on a large canvas in constantly changing light is always difficult, and I should have been wiser to have made a series of water-colour studies and then worked from these in the studio at home. However, the mischief was done, as I fully

realized when we got home and I unpacked the thing. I was horrified at the mess I had made, and spent days trying to pull it together. When it was alongside the other 'Creswicks' at the exhibition of student's work in December, I felt acutely what a dismal failure it was, though it was not, I think, quite the worst entry.

Every half-year there was a scholarship examination at the Schools and a fresh influx of students. The newcomers were always objects of interest. I had observed this when I was a new boy myself, working on probation, and some of the older students had come to inspect us. I learned later that after one of these visitations a senior girl student had burst into her painting class protesting, 'Have you seen the new lot? There's a boy of twelve! What *is* the place coming to?' I am sure I was the boy in question, for though I was seventeen I

was very small for my age, a fact which earned me the name of
'Little' Shepard.

It was while working in the back painting school that I first saw
Florence Chaplin. I was copying the Philip of Spain by Velasquez
when she came in with another girl and stood watching me at work.
I had heard her spoken of as being one of the cleverest students, a
distinction she shared with Flora Lion. Florence Chaplin's talent was
inherited from her grandfather, Ebenezer Landells, the artist and
engraver and one of the founders of *Punch*. I felt very conscious of
my poor painting and turning to her said, 'I am afraid I am not
making a very good job of it.' 'No. It is difficult,' she replied, 'but
I think you're frightened of it. Try painting more thickly.' She went
on: 'The drawing's all right but don't worry about going over the
edges.' It was the only advice I had received so far, and I thanked
her, explaining rather lamely that I had learned no oil painting and
was trying to find a method. I always remembered what she told
me. It cheered me up to be noticed and encouraged by her and
sometimes to be greeted by a quick smile when I passed her in the
corridor. It was nearly two years before I got to know her well,
for the men and women did not work or lunch together as had
happened at Heatherley's.

I had my own particular friends among the men. Philip Streatfeild was my own age, and altogether bigger. He was always cheerful,
and being endowed with a good voice often led us in song while
we were cleaning up in the wash-house after work. Our music was
of quite a high order and sung in parts, with Gilbert Holiday,
Denholm Davis and Stanley Young providing baritone and bass.
The corridors rang with 'Holy, Holy, Holy' or 'The Song of Praise'
most afternoons at 3.15. George Swaish, who entered the Schools
the year after I did, came from the West Country. It was he who

taught me how to fill my pipe. He was diffident and shy, and it was some time before I came to know him well. He was one of the most single-hearted men I have known, and of my friends the truest.

At the end of my first year I duly passed into the Upper School. There was no more drawing from the antique: it was painting, painting all the time, with a visiting Royal Academician to teach us. Some of this teaching was good and some quite the reverse. Marcus Stone, for instance, would lay down the law, discoursing on 'a sense of fatty sweetness' which was quite in keeping with the subjects of his pictures. G. H. Boughton, who favoured Dutch scenes of the seventeenth century – fancy-costumed figures skating – would seize my favourite brush and grind it on to the canvas so that it spread out fanwise, and then tell me to go ahead. We had Seymour Lucas and Arthur Hacker and several others. Solomon J. Solomon was an infrequent visitor, but he did teach us something.

It was quite different when Sargent was the visitor. He was dynamic. Bursting with energy and enthusiasm, he inspired us all. Everyone tried to paint as he did. On one occasion he seized palette and brushes from a student and got to work himself. The painting remained untouched after he had left and was taken home by the lucky student, though several of us tried to bribe him to part with it.

George Clausen was quite as popular as Sargent, though of a different temperament. A rather shy, quiet man, almost diffident in his criticisms, he was a most excellent teacher besides being a distinguished painter. I think he enjoyed being among students, for one day he joined us in the yard outside the Schools, where Arthur Connor took a photograph of us all.

The same autumn we heard that the fate of our home in Hammersmith had been finally decided. The whole of Theresa Terrace was to be pulled down forthwith. My secret hopes that the place might be saved were completely dashed and there was nothing to do but to make the best of it. Father and Ethel had been house-hunting for some time and the most favoured place was Blackheath, in southeast London. Father was attracted to Blackheath because he had been to school there before he went to Rugby; moreover, it was high and said to be bracing, which was considered good for rheumatic sufferers. It certainly was bracing, especially in winter, as we found out when crossing the heath with a north-east wind blowing. Cyril and I were not very enthusiastic about the choice; we thought it too far out of Town. However, Father told us one day that he had bought the lease of a house in Shooters Hill Road, and the following Saturday we made the journey to Blackheath to see it. The train from Charing Cross was slow but the walk across the heath was pleasant. No. 34 was a semi-detached house with a good garden, large enough, I was pleased to see, for a tennis court. The rooms were large and had a good basement. But there was no studio. I went to the top of the house, hoping to find a suitable room. Finally I decided that the spare room was the only possible place, though even this, cluttered up as it soon would be with a large double bed, a wardrobe and a washstand, did not seem very promising.

We took a lot of measurements, and found the ground-floor

rooms were high enough to take the Georgian mahogany bookcases which were a fitment in our house in Theresa Terrace and which Father was determined to save from the housebreakers. It was some compensation to find that we should have electric light instead of the oil lamps and gas we had been used to. The local builder met us at the house and arrangements were made to start redecoration.

Both Cyril and I were much concerned about our daily journey to Town, for the trains were not good, though he could get to Cannon Street more easily than I could to Charing Cross.

We also felt that the house was too far from the shops, which Lizzie would not like. I did not take as much interest in the redecoration as I had done in that of our old home; in fact, I did not visit it again until we moved in one cold day in late autumn. The vans arrived early in the morning at Theresa Terrace and the bookcases

were carefully and safely moved and packed in with our furniture. Then we took the train to Black-heath.

It was cold waiting about in an empty house for our furniture to arrive, and this added to the de-pression and unhappiness I already felt at leaving our old home. Darkness came on, and still we waited. Finally, overcome with hunger, we went in relays to the 'Sun in the Sands'

to warm ourselves with hot supper. It was nine o'clock before the vans came, and nearly midnight before all was unloaded and stowed in the house. The local policeman showed great interest in these proceedings. I believe he thought we were trying to 'shoot the moon'. But he got a drink and a tip and all was well. Lizzie arrived next day without her beloved cat, which had died some weeks earlier . . . no doubt some instinct had warned it of the coming upheaval.

Our two bookcases were duly fixed up in the dining-room and Ethel began the work of sorting and arranging our books. She enjoyed doing this; she was studying literature at Queen's College and spent a lot of time in the library there. It was her third year at the College and she was making good progress, besides keeping up her piano playing. She told us that the College was holding a reunion of old girls, and that she was particularly anxious to go in the hope that she might meet some of Mother's old friends. When the day arrived Father went with her and they both returned in great excitement. They had met Gussie and Poppie Tucker, two of Mother's friends. Gussie, whose full name was Augustine Boucneau, had been at the College with Mother, and they had kept up the friendship until Mother's death. We remembered Gussie from our early childhood and the lovely presents she used to give us at Christmas and on our birthdays. We had not seen or heard of her for eight years. She was now married to Groby Rogers and lived at Kingswear in south Devon. A warm invitation had been given us to visit her in her new home in the following spring. I was particularly glad about this as I had never been to Devonshire, and, indeed, on only one occasion had I ever seen the country in the springtime.

Cyril and I bombarded Ethel with questions about Gussie and her husband. It seems that he was smaller than she, and having spent much of his life in South Africa was very bronzed. The other college friend of Mother's, Poppy Tucker, I remembered well. Poppy had grey eyes and a mop of red hair – most attractive in my eyes. She had very little use for the conventions, and used to startle Harley Street by riding to College on horseback. She married a solicitor named Godefroi, and when his health broke she nursed him devotedly until he died. She was then left very badly off. I am glad to say that several years later I had a letter from her, characteristically short and to the point:

'Dear Ernest,

Rejoice with me. I have won seventeen thou' in the Irish Sweep. Now, of course, long lost relations are buzzing around like flies.'

Chapter Eleven

HOLIDAYS IN DEVON
AND GERMANY

SECOND-YEAR students who had passed into the Upper School
and could show a record of regular attendance and good behaviour were given certain privileges. Amongst these was the
chance to compete for a scholarship called 'The Landseer' which was
worth £40 a year for two years. Without telling Father I entered
three works – a study of a head, a painting of a nude, and a drawing.
It was a pleasant surprise for him, as for me, when I won the scholarship. Fred Appleyard won another scholarship at the same time.

Forty pounds for two years seemed to me a fortune. I could not
help remembering how I had won my first shilling at the age of
seven and had contemplated matrimony with Vera Beringer on the
strength of it. Since then my sense of proportion had improved, and
although now 'passing rich on £40 a year', I felt that matrimony was
not yet in sight. I had from time to time earned a few pounds by
making joke drawings at the rate of 5s. a drawing for a paper called
British Boys, and had even tried my luck without success with *Punch*.
So when an invitation came from Gussie I was able to tell Father that
I could pay my own fare to Devonshire.

Cyril, of course, could not go, being tied to the City until the
time came for his annual holiday; Ethel and I went together. We
were up early and, reaching Paddington before 10.30, took our seats
in a through carriage to Kingswear. I had never travelled on the

Great Western before, though I had studied much of its history, and had always loved its engines of dark green with shining brass-work. Great Western rolling stock, too, solidly built with cream-coloured uppers, the company's arms emblazoned on the panel and with clerestory windows, appealed to my aesthetic sense.

We settled ourselves in comfort and on the strength of my new-found wealth I booked two places for lunch in the dining-car. The main line through Westbury had not yet been built and we travelled via Bath and Bristol, stopping at each place. I knew the landmarks on the line from my study of the G.W.R. – the Box Tunnel, Clifton Suspension Bridge seen in the distance, and the flat lands before Taunton. After leaving Exeter we ran close to the sea by Dawlish, then turned inland again. The countryside with its red earth and bright spring green and its cider-apple orchards in bloom impressed me deeply and I realized why Devon had earned its title of Glorious.

As we neared Kingswear we came in sight of the Dart, with H.M.S. *Britannia* and H.M.S. *Hindustani* lying at anchor. The old three-deckers, painted black and white, were still the homes of the naval cadets, for the Royal Naval College had yet to be built.

As the train drew up at the quayside station at Kingswear I saw Gussie on the platform and beside her a small man with a fox terrier on a lead. 'That man must be Mr Rogers,' I thought. Gussie looked just the same as I remembered her nine years before: it was such a joy greeting her after all that time.

As we left the station she crossed the road and stopped at a baker's shop opposite. When she came out she told us we could leave our bags there and Mr Luckraft would bring them up when he delivered the bread. It was over a mile walk from the station to 'Coombeside' and a most delightful walk it was. Tropical trees and plants grew on the slopes down to the harbour and on the other side was the tiny church of St Petrox and the battery of obsolete guns. Groby Rogers and I walked behind the others and he pointed out the blue gum trees. Blue gum trees, he told me, grew to an immense size in South Africa. He was a quiet little man, but he had a gay twinkle in his eye and I took to him immediately.

Coombeside stood by itself on the side of a little valley running down to the sea, with a tiny cove at the bottom. There was a very small landing-stage cut into the rocks and a boat was hanging from davits. We left the road and turned into a drive bordered with bracken and ferns. The house had a pleasant loggia with french windows and a grand view across the bay to Start Point. I was quite enchanted by it.

After tea Mr Luckraft arrived with our bags and sundry groceries and bread for Groby's brother, Harry Rogers, who lived in an isolated house across the valley. Neither the baker nor the postman liked the extra walk that delivery entailed, so an arrangement was made whereby things were brought to Coombeside and collected

from time to time. Groby and I sorted the parcels and packed two baskets, Gussie's voice reminding us from upstairs: 'Don't forget the bottle of whisky and his letters. And there's a bag of saffron buns – he likes those.'

We sallied forth. A footpath down the hill brought us to the cove. Snap the fox terrier followed close at heel as he had been trained to do since, a year before, while chasing rabbits among the bracken, he

136

had been bitten by an adder. 'I saw him standing with his tongue out and whimpering,' said Groby, 'and I went across to him. I guessed what had happened immediately I saw the tiny red marks on his paw, and I ran home with him as fast as I could. Fortunately I had had experience of snake-bites and knew what to do. The dog's leg was swelling so I slashed the paw with a razor until it bled freely and then poured in whisky. He was all right in a couple of days. But it was a near thing.'

From the cove we climbed a hill by a rough cart-track and came in sight of a small house close to the edge of the cliff. It had a very untidy garden and a little greenhouse. There was a young man at work in an outhouse on some carpentry. Groby hailed him: 'Hullo, Herbert. Is Harry in?' The young man stopped work and jerked his thumb over his shoulder. Harry Rogers appeared round a corner and greeted us. He was short, like his brother, but more lightly built and his fair hair was thin on top. We had difficulty in entering the

house, for the porch was stacked with planks of various sizes. We climbed over a carpenter's saw-bench and entered a large sitting-room. The place was covered in shavings and looked like a carpenter's shop, though there was a carpet on the floor. By way of explanation, Harry waved his hand towards the mess and said: 'You see, we are getting

on with the big organ.' This statement surprised and puzzled me, for there was already an organ, a small one of somewhat original design, in the corner of the room. I was soon to learn the workings of this extraordinary *ménage*. Harry was a very keen musician, and Herbert, who showed musical promise, had been more or less adopted by him and he was teaching the lad to play. But Herbert, in addition to his musical gifts, had proved to be handy with carpenter's tools, and between them Harry and Herbert had designed and built the small organ in the sitting-room. This instrument had a wonderful tone and it was a great treat for me to listen to the music which young Herbert produced from it. Now the pair were building a larger organ – hence the clutter. I was shown the drawings for the new instrument and was taken to the outhouse where the boy was lovingly fashioning the tiny wood-and-leather valves. Both men were wildly enthusiastic about their plans, and it was difficult to bring Harry down to earth sufficiently to give us his next grocery order.

In earlier days Herbert had rigged the dinghy we had seen down in the cove. Several times we went sailing in it in Dartmouth Bay, where the pilot boat lay at anchor waiting for an incoming ship. There were two pilot boats. We called them 'Penny' and 'Twopenny' because they bore 1D and 2D painted on their sails. One evening when we came back from a sail Harry Rogers was waiting in the cove. After the boat was stowed away he said to me: 'You know, I always feel a little anxious till Herbert gets back. He handles the boat perfectly – but you never know. I can never forget what happened three years ago.' Then he told me how two cadets from H.M.S. *Britannia* had come with the Vicar from Dartmouth in their sailing-boat. They had all had tea up at his house and at about six o'clock left to sail back. As the Vicar had to make a call at Kingswear the boys started alone. They knew how to handle the boat and were perfectly at home with her, and it was but a short distance to the harbour, so no one entertained qualms. Harry told me he watched the boys leave the cove and saw them wave to him as they passed out of sight round the headland. No trace of them or of the boat was ever found. Harry, his eyes full of tears, turned to me and said: 'I can never now bear to watch our boat round the headland.'

The evenings were chilly and after supper we sat round the fire at Coombeside. Groby lay on the settee in the corner with Snap curled up beside him, while Gussie showed us some of her special treasures. She talked to us of her schooldays with Mother at Queen's College. She explained, with slight embarrassment, why she had found it difficult to keep in touch with us since Mother's death. She had once met the Aunts during Mother's lifetime and had not got on well with them. This did not surprise us, for indeed Mother herself, with all her tact and sweet nature, had found it difficult to adjust herself to the conditions of Gordon Square. But now that we were with her again Gussie's friendship was to be unbroken till her death in 1922.

Took pot-shots at rabbits

Groby and I took long walks, with Snap at our heels, over toward
Brownstone and the Beacon. We usually carried a ·22 rifle and took
pot-shots at rabbits – not easy to hit with a rifle. We once went as
far as Man sands under Berry Head, where it seemed Groby had
sometimes found gold quartz. Having spent years digging for gold
in South Africa he knew what to look for. Grubbing about among
the stones, he pocketed a few to take home and break up with his
hammer. He told me he had sent specimens to London to be assayed,
but the analysis, though it showed traces of gold, did not offer much
prospect of a fortune. He had been in the Transvaal during the un-
settled times preceding the Boer War, and had always been in
trouble with the Boers. He made me a present of some garnets that
he had scooped up in the Vaal River while he was being shot at by
a Boer farmer.

My visit to Devon had a profound effect on me. It seemed to open
a new chapter in my life. Much of the happiness that I had felt when
Mother was alive returned to me. Groby's friendship, which seemed
to grow with the years, was a tonic to me and helped me to overcome a certain aloofness to which I was prone and which he chaffed
me out of by calling me 'Grandpa'.

Groby and Gussie had known each other since childhood. At
sixteen he had left home and gone to Russia, but he did not like it
there and soon returned. Then, when the gold rush started in South
Africa, off he went to make his fortune. He found gold all right, but
not enough, and was soon on his beam-ends. He lived with the Zulus
in a kraal for more than a year, learning their language and even
translating 'Three Blind Mice' into Zulu. This, 'Matatu eibooni
goondarni', was adopted by the young warriors as a war song.
Groby, suitably clad and armed with a knobkerrie, would then give
us a rendering of it, while Gussie shook with laughter and Snap

barked. I learned most of the song by heart and gave a performance of it later in the corridor at the Schools – till the noise brought the Keeper on the scene.

I think that Father must have had a windfall about this time, for one evening in July he surprised us by asking if we would like to go to Germany for our summer holiday. Would we not! Cyril's holiday was due in the last fortnight of August, and our plans were made accordingly. On a Saturday in the middle of the month we found ourselves at Liverpool Street station boarding the train for Harwich. I was determined to try my hand at oil painting again and had packed my easel, camp-stool and two or three canvases. We arrived at Harwich in the late afternoon and went on board S.S. *Peregrine*. She was not an inviting-looking ship. Painted black all over, she had none of the attraction of our friend *Tamise* of two years before.

It was a thirty-two-hour voyage and the third-class sleeping quarters were in the bowels of the ship and very stuffy. Soon after leaving harbour we began to pitch and roll. Dinner was eaten in ominous silence, and Father hurried from the table before the end of the meal. I went on deck, but it was so cold that I soon took refuge in the saloon. A few men were drinking there. Ethel had disappeared. It was not long before Cyril and I too were stricken down. The dreadful atmosphere below and the signs of distress all around were our final undoing. I spent a miserable night; I had not realized

sea-sickness could be so pain-ful. I lay on the hard bunk and longed for the end of the world. In the morning Cyril went on deck, but was down again almost immediately – the smell of frying bacon was too much for him. I tried to face food at lunch-time, but in vain. Ethel, however, was by now quite cheerful; she had recovered from her attack, and she ate a hearty meal. There was no sign of Father. We had none of us seen him since he left the dinner-table the previous evening. A search revealed him lying on a settee in the third-class saloon wrapped in a rug and, mercifully, asleep. By sundown my inside was beginning to settle down and, after we had passed Heligo-land and run into calmer waters, I fancied I could face a meal. Alas! I still couldn't. Feeling I had been stretched on the rack, I retired again to my bunk.

I awoke next morning to sounds of activity and the rattling of chains. Looking out of the porthole I saw that the ship was alongside a quay, which I realized must be Hamburg. By this time Cyril and I were clamorous for food. We waited very impatiently for breakfast to be served and ate heartily when we got it. Father was up, but feeling squeamish; and it was not, indeed, until he got his feet on dry land again that he recovered his equilibrium.

After very brief formalities we boarded a train for Hildesheim. It was a dull journey: flat, featureless countryside for miles and miles;

but the old town, when we reached it, was a pleasant contrast. The streets were lined with red-brick and timbered houses, many with signs hanging over the pavement. A narrow river, running through the centre of the town, gave it an almost Dutch appearance. We chose an hotel from Baedeker and it proved cheap and comfortable. The German meals were excellent. It was something new to have stewed, syrupy fruit with our meat, and rich pastries with cream to follow, but I could have done without the caraway seeds. For breakfast we had honey and delicious hot rolls.

The German people interested me greatly. The tradesmen seemed to have distinctive clothes – a square white cap for a carpenter, a top hat for a sweep. There were many soldiers in the streets and when they passed an officer they broke into the goose step, slapping the pavement with their feet. Everything in the town was very orderly and well kept, which gave the place a prosperous air. I chose a spot near the river and painted the red houses overhanging the water while Father made sketches in the church near by.

We stayed five days at Hildesheim and then moved on to Wernigerode, a dull place on the River Oder. From Wernigerode we took a trip to the Brocken. A light railway took us to the top of this so-called mountain. We passed numerous signs with 'AN DER SCHÖNEN AUSSICHT', but I could see nothing very beautiful, nor was the view from the summit impressive. Even the witches were absent – except on the postcards on sale in large numbers at a kiosk.

We did not stay long at the top, but on our way down we came to a beer garden. It looked inviting, with a waterfall in the background and coloured plaster gnomes lurking in the surrounding pinewoods, so we chose a table and sat down. The waterfall interested me; it had a suspiciously artificial look and presently Cyril and I slipped away to investigate it. We found a path that led up to the rocks above the fall and there saw that a natural stream had been diverted into a channel made to carry the water over the edge. Peering down, we could see the beer garden below with a family party gathered at each table. We decided to stop the waterfall. Collecting a number of large stones, we gradually filled up the diversion channel. Retracing our steps, we joined Father and Ethel, and we did not have to wait long before signs of consternation became evident. Stout gentlemen forsaking their beer stood pointing upwards; a waiter was sent to fetch the manager. The water diminished to a trickle and voices were raised calling for an explanation. Cyril and I quietly told Father what we had done and we all decided it was time to go. As we left, the manager, a portly man, was being assisted up the steep path by two waiters.

After three days we went on to Goslar. This delightful mediaeval town provided a complete contrast to Wernigerode. It was surrounded by a wall with gates and round bastions roofed with tiles. In the centre of the square stood a fountain topped with a bronze eagle which, it was said, dated from the tenth century. Opposite was a picturesque old inn where we inquired for rooms. Herr Bode, the proprietor, greeted us and found us accommodation, and then broached the subject of dinner. 'You will have some nice trouts, yes?' We were shown the fish swimming in a tank. Delicious trout they proved to be.

Goslar was a garrison town and there were plenty of soldiers

about. The officers of artillery were particularly smart in their dark-blue frock-coats with red facings. Apparently it was a good thing for civilian pedestrians to step aside into the road when officers passed on the side-walks; the demigods of the army were treated with immense respect in the Kaiser's Germany. A corner of the dining-room at our inn was set aside for their use. No civilian ever violated the sanctity of these tables.

The bronze fountain in the square interested me deeply and I made some drawings of it. The eagle on top was a quaint bird like a soda-water bottle with wings. Water spouted from its beak. In the evening the young men and maidens gathered round it. The girls, many with fair hair plaited in twin pigtails, were wearing national dress of full skirt and short black embroidered bodice. There were no cinemas to draw young people indoors in those days.

We could not stay long in Goslar, for our fortnight was nearly over. On leaving we spent a night at Harzburg, a spa with little of interest, before moving on to Brunswick for our last night in Germany. Father had chosen from the bottom of Baedeker's list an hotel which seemed likely to be the cheapest in the city. When, however, we left the railway station and asked for it, we were directed to a smart bus which landed us at a most imposing building though on an ugly site. It appeared that Baedeker's cheap hotel had been rebuilt and was now one of the best

and most expensive. Father tackled the manager, who promised to accommodate us at a reasonable figure as this was the off season. We escaped the next day, dodging the staff lined up in the hall and slinking out by a side entrance with the connivance of the under-porter.

Our arrival back at Hamburg was marked by a full-scale thunderstorm. The lightning, like streamers from clouds to earth, was an impressive sight as we sailed down the river. The deluge of rain seemed to have a quieting effect on the sea, for the return voyage was a placid one. In the afternoon Ethel entertained the passengers with a concert on the ship's antediluvian piano. Owing to our shortage of cash care had to be exercised in our choice of meals, but by pooling our resources we were just able to pay our fares back to Blackheath.

That autumn a debating society was formed at the Royal Academy Schools. The meetings were not always given to formal debates, sometimes a paper was read. As I listened I began to realize the deficiencies of my education. I had never been a diligent reader and now found myself far behind my fellow students in knowledge of English prose and poetry. The Society's meetings were held in the evenings, usually at a room in New Court normally used as a studio by two of the girls. Afterwards Philip Streatfeild and I would go out of our way to see Florence Chaplin and her sister Adrienne, also a student, to their home in Earl's Court.

The time was coming for the winter show of students' work. The prize-giving that followed was always held on the tenth of December, Foundation Day of the Royal Academy, and also, as it happened, my birthday. Our paintings and drawings were hung in the Academy Galleries, and we were able to criticize and appraise each other's work and decide which were likely to be prize-winners. The painting about which we were all agreed that year was the head of a girl in profile by Florence Chaplin; it was quite outstanding. When we were all in the Gallery I went up to her and said how good I thought it was: we walked over and stood before it. Then she said: 'I got into trouble with the Visitor, you know. He accused me of putting palette scrapings on the hair.' She gave me one of her quick smiles and added, 'He was horrified when I admitted it.' She asked to see my work, which, as no signatures were allowed, she had been unable to identify. She stood in front of it for a few moments and said, 'Your drawing is much better than your painting. You are still afraid of your paint.' 'Yes, I know,' I replied, 'I only wish you would give me a lesson.' 'Oh! I couldn't do that. I have never taught painting and should not know where to begin.' When the prize-winners were announced, Florence, to my joy, was given the silver medal.

After Christmas we made up a party to see the pantomime at

Drury Lane Pantomime, drawn at aged 13

Drury Lane. Cyril and I had been to every pantomime there for several years. No longer were Dan Leno and Herbert Campbell the main attractions as they had been for nearly ten years. Some of the best contemporary comedians had been substituted, but the effect was not the same and everyone missed the famous pair. We paid our half-crowns and fought our way into the pit. I cannot recall which of the small range of traditional pantomime stories this one was supposed to represent, but I do remember Harry Randall, robust and loud of voice, singing

> *Oh what a happy land is England!*
> *Envied by all nations near and far.*
> *Though of Gladstone we're bereft,*
> *We have Winston Churchill left.*
> *Oh what a happy land we are.*

Churchill was even then making his name – one of the angry young men at the turn of the century.

Chapter Twelve

MY FIRST STUDIO

Iᴺ England the year 1899 ended in gloom. The Boer War had
started and after some initial successes the situation of the British
troops had rapidly deteriorated. None of our generals was prepared for the elusive tactics of the Boer. They had never had to face
an enemy armed with modern weapons, and their hidebound
approach to their problems only led to the destruction of their
troops. There were plenty of armchair tacticians to tell them how
the war should be fought, but the wretched struggle dragged on for
three years. Much bitter feeling existed in the country and outspoken
criticism was uttered on all sides. In the schools we had many
arguments about the rights and wrongs of the war. In spite of my
love of soldiering I could not work up any enthusiasm and never
felt the slightest impulse to volunteer for the Imperial Yeomanry.

With the New Year things began to look more promising, and
when the news came of the relief of Ladysmith, followed by that of
Mafeking, we really let ourselves go. The students of the Royal
College of Art prepared a celebration in the form of a procession
through the West End of London with a statue of Queen Victoria.
The statue, larger than life, was constructed in a most ingenious
way devised by the professor of sculpture. The seated figure was
built up on a wooden foundation; the head and shoulders, an excellent
likeness, were modelled in clay and placed on top; and old curtains
were arranged as draperies and sprayed with plaster. The whole was
placed on a large sculptor's trolley and looked most imposing.

On the appointed day the students sallied forth in their painting smocks, some of dark blue, and moved down Bond Street to meet the procession coming along Piccadilly. (Next day a paragraph in one of the daily newspapers commented: 'It was a strange sight to see a procession of butchers marching down Bond Street and turning

into Piccadilly.') When we Academy Schools students joined up with the procession, intermittent bursts of cheering encouraged our journey along Piccadilly. At the Circus we turned up Regent Street. It was a fine sight looking back from the head of the procession: fifty or sixty smocked students straining at the ropes of the trolley with the girls marching behind waving palms. It looked rather like some scene from the building of the Pyramids. There were no traffic difficulties; the police just held everything up and let us go by. We had no band, but we broke into song at intervals and were much cheered by the crowd.

At the Schools we had also our own small celebrations. These took place in the evenings when we were working in the life class, and were often staged for the express purpose of ragging the Curator. He was a plump, unctuous man named Bosdet, with a neat little beard and a manner that did not commend itself. On one occasion we formed a procession after assembling in the corridor. I got myself up as Kruger in a borrowed top hat and a Newgate frill made of cotton wool. We entered the classroom singing a funeral dirge. This

was too much for Bosdet. He rushed to the door to bar our progress. There was a short struggle and he was borne backwards, his cries of 'Gentlemen! gentlemen!' becoming fainter until, breathless, he sank into his seat. Mopping his brow he gasped: 'I shall report you for this. It is quite easy to see it is an organized disturbance.' He was still fretting and fuming when the visiting Academician appeared in the doorway. It was the American artist Edwin Abbey and he was wearing his top hat (my 'Kruger' one was stowed away under my seat). This was no coincidence, for Abbey went everywhere in his hat, though he usually removed his jacket. As Bosdet fussed up to him and poured into his ear the tale of our misdoings a broad grin spread over Abbey's face, and looking round he said, 'Waal, they seem quiet enough now,' as indeed we were and hard at work too. Nothing much came of the affair except that the Keeper, Crofts, came in the next evening and read us a little homily ending, in an undertone, with 'You must try not to annoy Mr Bosdet, you know.'

We were always glad when Abbey was the Visitor. Not only was he a brilliant draughtsman and a great teacher, but he took a continuing interest in our welfare. I had him to thank for my introduction to *Punch* four years later, while several of his other students were employed by him at his studio at Fairford when he was painting the big frescoes for the Boston Library. I never could see the object of the Curator's presence at the evening life class. On the rare occasions when Bosdet was away and the Keeper appointed a senior student to take charge, perfect quiet was preserved and no one thought of making a disturbance.

In the early part of the summer I devoted some weeks to working for a British Institution prize. This was a cash prize of £60 a year for two years and was open to students all over the kingdom. When the results were declared in July I was one of the lucky ones. This, added to my £40 from the Landseer Scholarship, would give me £100 for the next year, and I began to consider the possibility of taking a studio in town, perhaps sharing it with another student. There was to be another competition for the Creswick Prize in the summer and I wanted to paint my picture in Devon, where I knew of a subject close to my friends at Kingswear.

Philip Streatfeild and I decided to go together, so I wrote to Gussie and she found us rooms in a labourer's cottage in their valley, for which we each paid one pound a week all in. Early in August we travelled down together. Again Gussie, Groby and Snap met us at the station and Mr Luckraft's cart transported our luggage. We had the tiniest rooms, but Mrs Blake looked after us well. Within a few days we had begun our painting. Usually we worked until midday, when Groby would appear at the top of the valley and join us for a bathe in the cove.

It was a perfect summer. In Devon we had four weeks of

unbroken sunshine. The use of Harry's dinghy, he and Herbert being away on the moors, was a special amenity, and we also had the run of his home, 'The Warren'. Philip was a pianist, so we had some

gay evenings at the house on the cliff. There were plenty of mackerel about and our painting was often inter- rupted by Groby shouting down the valley that the fish were in the bay. We would leave our work and launch the dinghy

in no time and go off to chase the shoals. We caught dozens at a time. Sometimes we did not even need to use the boat, for the mackerel would come right into the cove, chasing the little britt which made for the rocks, and we could scoop the fish out with our hands. It was great fun grabbing the mackerel and throwing them up on the rocks. We had them for supper most nights. There are few things nicer than mackerel grilled fresh from the sea.

Regatta week came to Dartmouth at the end of the month. There were three nights of it, with fireworks to round it off. The whole harbour front was given over to merry-go-rounds, swings and sideshows. Old Hancock sat in front of the big centre tent waving the crowd in, and gnawing great hunks of meat on the bone. Two dancing girls in short tight-waisted spangled skirts and high boots danced to the rhythm of the mechanical organ. The woman at the

pay desk examined our hands to see if we could pass as workers and so get cheaper seats. The yachting folk, ashore from their craft, mingled with the crowds and would give a golden sovereign to the roundabout man for a whole evening's turn.

Though I had not finished my competition painting, I left after the Fair to join Father, Ethel and Cyril in Suffolk. They were staying at Wade's Farm, near Dunwich, and I was eager to go there as I knew that not far away, at Hinton, I should find Florence Chaplin. She had told me earlier in the year that her mother had a house there and that she and her sister would probably be at Hinton in the summer. I spent a night in London with my two aunts in Gordon Square. It was the last time I was to stay there, for Aunt Alicia, my godmother, died the following winter and the house was sold. Next day I took train to Saxmundham, where Cyril met me on a hired bicycle. After fixing my bag on the back of my own machine, we pedalled the four miles to Wade's Farm. It was a lonely place and not very attractive, but near enough to Dunwich to get some bathing. I felt very nervous about presenting myself at the Red House, the Chaplins' home, and as Cyril was coming with me we decided to

arrive at three o'clock so that no meal would be involved. I need not have worried. We were given a warm welcome, and I was terribly flattered when Florence introduced me to her mother with, 'This is little Shepard. You have heard of him.'

Besides four girls

there was a brother, Lindsay, whom I remembered as a small boy, even smaller than I, at St Paul's; he was still at school. Florence and her younger sister had their hair done in pigtails and with short skirts looked almost like schoolgirls. We were made to stay to tea and the girls cycled part of the way back with us. I think Cyril was as taken with Adrienne as I was with her sister, and I know we were a couple of very gay young men when we reached the farm. Within a few days it became a settled thing for us to cycle over to the Red House and call for the girls to join us in an outing.

We had to go home at the end of a fortnight for Cyril's holiday was up and I had to go back to Devonshire to finish my picture. This time I stayed at Coombeside and worked in the spare room, for the weather had turned too cold and wet for outdoor work. The Academy term had already started, so after a week I had to say goodbye to Gussie and Groby and make for home.

Once back at the Schools I gave my serious attention to the problem of sharing a studio and was turning over in my mind whom I should ask when the matter was settled for me. George Swaish came up to me while we were washing our brushes and said, rather diffidently, 'I hear you are thinking of sharing a studio. Would you think of sharing with me?' I had never considered George as a possible, and was a bit startled, for I did not, as yet, know him well, but I agreed at once. I am very glad I did so, for it was really the start of our friendship, a friendship that lasted till his death in 1930. I learned from him much that helped to broaden my outlook on life.

We did not waste any time but started studio-hunting forthwith. We saw dozens, large and small, sound and leaky, and eventually settled on No. 52 Glebe Place, Chelsea. It was large with enough space for two to work. It had a tiny bedroom, big enough for two truckle beds, an adequate lavatory, a larder and a coalhole. The care-taker, Mrs Scott, lived next door and was prepared to do what cleaning was necessary. The rent was £50 per annum, £10 more than we meant to pay, but we agreed that as George would have to give up his digs and make it his home, something good was practicable. We took the studio from the Christmas quarter. As my twenty-first birthday was on December 10th, I was able to make it known to those interested that presents in the form of pieces of furniture would be most acceptable. As a result I received a studio easel from Frank Dicksee, an armchair from his sister, and Gussie, dear Gussie, wrote to say I could have her piano if transport could be arranged.

George and I went shopping. We bought our beds and bedding at Maple's, which gave customers a free lunch in those days. We bought pots and pans and a small gas-cooker in the King's Road,

and invited Cyril and Philip Streatfeild to join us in our first meal. We chose a steak, and as I knew steaks had to be beaten, I laid ours on a drawing-board and hammered it with a T-square. It came out quite thin, like a small blanket, and had to be folded several times to get it into the pan. We fried some onions and potato chips and the meal was washed down with bottled beer. The steak was as tough as hide.

I arranged that I would live at the studio during the week and go home for week-ends. George and I developed a regular breakfast drill: one shaved while the other stood by to see that the porridge didn't boil over. It was great fun. Sometimes we were joined by Arthur Connor on his way to Heatherley's. I was rather concerned about Arthur: I felt he was getting into a rut. He had been at Heatherley's over three years, and seemed quite content to spend the rest of his life there. George and I felt this would never do, and we joined in a determined effort to persuade him to try for a scholarship at the Academy Schools. At first he only dug in his heels, saying he was doing quite well where he was. But in the end we secured his consent. He passed, and in due course joined us as a student.

I found studio life very pleasant. When we had finished work in the evening life-class three or four of us would have a meal together. It had to be somewhere cheap, and we found a suitable

restaurant in the Brompton Road, close to the Oratory, a place patronized chiefly by cab-men. We sat round a table with a zinc top and ordered meat and two vegetables for 6d. When we were in funds we followed this with apple turnover. The serving girl was called Polly, and she always giggled when we called for 'Turnover, Polly!' A small man with a large expressionless face was part of the establishment. He seemed to spend his life washing the floor, and was usually out of sight under a table. After a particularly bright sally on our part his face would appear like a full moon, only to duck again immediately he was observed.

We held a house-warming party in the New Year. The piano had arrived and Philip Streatfeild played. Both the Chaplin girls were there; Father and Ethel came up from Blackheath; and everyone brought a small gift. Father's arthritis was now acute and even the short journey from Blackheath tried him.

About this time we began to hear disquieting rumours of the Queen's state of health. References to her condition in the press were at first guarded, but presently it became apparent that the old lady was failing rapidly. But although the public was to some extent prepared for the news of her death when it occurred on January 22nd the effect on us all was strangely contradictory. Somehow we had almost come to believe that she could go on for ever. The whole country mourned, people going about with bowed heads. The funeral procession through London was a very moving sight. George and I stood amongst the crowd in Sussex Place to see it pass. King Edward and the Kaiser followed immediately behind the coffin, which was borne on a gun-carriage. It was all very simple; only the bands playing the funeral march broke the silence. No one could fail to mark the difference from the cheering crowds of three years earlier.

After my mother's death, Father had given up his connections with the theatrical world. This winter, however, he was asked to stage a Shakespearian play in aid of the hospital for sick children in Great Ormonde Street. In the past he had produced several plays for the Irving Club, and now he wrote to some of the members, friends with whom he had played, to enlist their support. Having had experience of the difficulties in managing the front of the house, he put that part of the business in charge of an agent. *Measure for Measure* was the play chosen. The club had produced it successfully some years previously and a cast of good amateur actors was formed. Cyril and I were given small parts; mine was Verges, and I much enjoyed it. A host of Academy students, male and female, was forthcoming for the 'crowds' and the dance in the last act. We had a very good orchestra, an organ for the marriage scene, and an ex-army drummer and bugler for 'tuckets off'. Some scenery was specially painted and Nathan provided the costumes. St George's Hall in Upper Regent Street was hired and *Punch*, a staunch supporter of the Children's Hospital, provided an ornamental programme. It was all the greatest fun.

Six months later we students produced another theatrical venture of quite a different kind. It was a burlesque of 'Sherlock Holmes' written by a student from Cope's school. I was cast for the lead;

I don't know why, for though I had grown a lot and was no longer 'little Shepard', I was hardly tall enough for Holmes. But by adding something to the heels of my boots (like Wilson Barrett in *The Sign of the Cross*) I gained sufficient height. Our studio in Glebe Place was used both for rehearsals and for scene-painting. We made a lot of mess with our backcloth for the scene in the *Twopenny Tube*. As a curtain-raiser we did W. W. Jacobs' *Ghost of Jerry Bundler*, and were lucky to get Charles Rock, the actor and dramatizer of the play, to produce it for us. The show was produced at the Queen's Gate Hall in Harrington Road and was received with great enthusiasm.

After all this excitement I settled down to work again. I persuaded Ethel to sit for me. It was an ordinary portrait, but it was accepted by the Royal Academy and hung on the line at the Summer Exhibition, the only success I have ever had with a portrait. I had little time for any other outside work as the conditions of my Landseer Scholarship entailed my regular attendance at the Schools either in the morning or the evening. However, I decided to enter for a landscape competition called the 'Turner', with a subject, announced early in the year, of a bridge over the Thames in London. I chose to paint Tower Bridge; I don't know why, for it is neither beautiful nor easy. In preparation I explored the dark alleys leading to the river round London Bridge and Blackfriars Bridge, but this proved vain, for the alleys, besides being smelly, were liable to inundation at high tide. Next I thought of trying a wharf. There were a great number to choose from, but I was lucky in meeting a man who advised me to try Hay's Wharf, which stands opposite the Tower of London. It was shut when I located it, but the night watchman answered my knocking. He assured me that there would be no trouble over my painting if I came after working hours. I explained that I had a large canvas and he agreed I could keep it in his watch-room. His name was Dan and I learned much about the riverside from him. He began by warning me to be careful how I went about, for lately there had been groups of young men, known as hooligans, who were causing trouble on the riverside and doing a lot of damage. He told me that only a few nights previously they had smashed a window in the wharf next door and stolen a lot of stuff. On his advice I carried my traps along before closing time, for he said that if the trouble-makers saw  my canvas as like as not they would poke a hole in it. For several weeks I worked every evening until the light failed without trouble or disturbance of any kind. Another warning Dan gave me was: 'Don't be seen talking to the police, else the lads'll be after you.' I had noticed that the police went about in couples and I was careful to avoid them. I often passed groups of hooligans lounging at street corners; gradually we got on nodding terms, and even got as far as exchanging good nights. Poor lads! They had nowhere to go to except the pubs. No wonder they got into mischief.

Chapter Thirteen

IN LOVE

Now that we had a piano at our studio, George and I decided we ought to make use of it, so we invited our friends to come for music in the evenings. I cleaned my fiddle, bought some new strings and, with Streatfeild at the piano, we tried our hands at simple things. Two or three others joined us, Denholm Davis came with his violin, Stanley Young the sculptor – Big Ben we called him – brought his 'cello, and Mortimer Brown, another sculptor, his flute. Gradually we became more ambitious and tackled Handel. Our rendering of the Largo was unorthodox but effective; we had no music for the 'cello and Big Ben had to improvise. The standard of chamber music we attained was not high, but it gave us

pleasure and we arranged to give a concert. We clubbed together and laid on a supper of bread and cheese and beer. Then we invited our men friends, adding a suggestion that anyone who could play, sing or recite would be called upon. The result was a variety programme. After a solemn start with the Largo and a song or two, Reginald Higgins gave some excellent impersonations, which were followed by a flute solo, 'Alice, where art thou?' by Mortimer Brown, and we wound up with a Zulu war dance. This brought the caretaker with a message of protest from the man next door.

Our studio grew to be a meeting-place for students of the neighbourhood. Besides Streatfeild at Trafalgar Studios, there was Gregory Robinson at the Onslow Warren in the King's Road. Gregory was perpetually hard up, and although he was a good marine painter he seldom had the luck to sell his paintings. His studio, at the top of that ramshackle block, was small and very untidy, with always the remains of a meal mixed up with the paints and brushes on the table. The room was lit by gas, and more than once we found Gregory struggling to work by candlelight for want of a shilling to put in the meter slot.

It was a great day for him when he was commissioned by a journal to make a double-page drawing of the return of the P. & O. liner from an Empire cruise with the Prince of Wales on board. The night was a foggy one when George and I decided to go round and see how Gregory was getting on with his picture. We found him working against time and almost in despair. He sat looking at his drawing. 'The bows, the bows!' he groaned. 'I can't get them right.' The thing had to be finished by the next morning and Gregory had had no dinner. First, then, he must be fed, so we hustled him out to get something to eat. Then we thought we might be able to help the picture along in his absence. Neither George nor I knew much about

ships, but even we could see that the bows were a bit odd. I remembered that there was a student who lived not far away who was an expert on ships and we decided to consult him. Off we went through the fog, found him at home, explained the situation, and brought him back with us. I can't remember his name, but I know that the first thing he said was, 'He's got the bows wrong.'

'Very well,' we said, 'that's what Gregory says himself. Put them right.'

'Oh! I couldn't do that,' he protested.

'You must,' was our answer. 'And quick – before Gregory comes back.'

He started work, and while he was busy at one end of the picture I went ahead at the other, painting the people in the boats waving to the ship, while George added flags, lots of them fluttering in the breeze. We were rather pleased with our combined efforts. When Gregory returned he sat down and stared. For a few minutes he said nothing; then: 'There's a story somewhere about fairies or mice doing something in the night, but I never knew mice who could draw ships.' He was not in the least put out, and agreed that the bows were better, but he did complain about my boatloads of people and George's display of bunting. We left him to carry on, and at about eleven the following morning he called at our studio with the picture under his arm on his way to Fleet Street. I hope they paid him adequately.

There was a lot of fog that winter. At times it was so thick that traffic practically ceased. This did not worry us because George and I always walked from the Schools to Chelsea. Sometimes Arthur Connor accompanied us, though he would never join us in dining at the 'Bug and Gluepot', as we called our haunt in the Brompton Road; he preferred to take his meal at home. One particularly foggy night we three started out from the Schools after the evening life-class. It was all right till we came to Hyde Park Corner. There it was so dense that we could not see the kerb and the lamps were dim yellow blurrs. Arthur, who had little sense of direction, bore off to the left and was lost to sight in a moment. I knew his failing and we decided he must be found at all costs. We called his name. No answer! Then, raising our voices, we shouted in unison. A faint cry of distress came out of the fog and we made for the sound. It was like navigating at sea with only the sound of a distant foghorn to guide us. The nearer we seemed to get the fainter became the bleats. Finally we struck (literally) the railings in Belgrave Square. We knew that our quarry could not be far off. Then George had a brain-wave. 'Let us,' he said, 'separate and go round the square in opposite directions, keeping to the railings, till we meet again on the other side.' I did not have to go far before I found Arthur. He was clinging to the railings thinking he was at Victoria Station. 'All right,' I bellowed at the top of my voice. 'He's found.' When we fore-gathered again we had to decide what action to take. It was out of the question to leave Arthur to his own devices, so we all made for Sloane Square, a simple job for those used to it. At the Underground we said good night to him and dived into an A.B.C. in the King's Road for some supper.

The Prize Distribution at the Academy Schools that winter was a really happy event for me. I had won a medal for a painted figure and ten pounds for a set of life drawings. But what pleased me even more was that Florence Chaplin had won the £40 Prize for a mural. The subject was 'The Procession of the Hours' and she treated it by showing the Horae as female figures. It was lovely both in colour and design and the award was a most popular one, all agreeing that it was by far the best. She was later to be commissioned to carry out

168

A group from the mural

the design for the nurses' dining-room at Guy's Hospital. It was a big undertaking, measuring twenty-five feet in length, and took her over a year to paint. Many years later I was able to buy back the original drawing, and it hangs in my drawing-room today.

At the prize distribution both my father and Mrs Chaplin were present. They sat together and got on extremely well: a couple of proud parents delighted at their children's successes. As Mrs Chaplin afterwards expressed it, 'Ready to burst with pride.'

After the gloom of Queen Victoria's death it was a relief when spring came to London. I worked at the Schools in the daytime, and started making studies for my riverside picture at Hay's Wharf in the evening. I did not begin work on the big canvas till the early summer, and as the days lengthened I was able to put in long hours at it. I was careful to follow Dan's advice, and never had any trouble with the hooligans.

When the Schools broke up in July George asked me to spend a

week at his home at Bristol. We agreed to make the journey by
cycle. It was a long haul – 120 miles – but we felt equal to it, especially
if we rode at night. By starting at about nine in the evening we should
reach Bristol by breakfast-time. I bought a valise to fit on my cycle
and packed a few clothes. We settled our accounts with the caretaker,
and on a warm night early in August we set off. I had told Florence
of our plans and she suggested that we call at her home in Earls
Court, which we did and were given packets of sandwiches and
were waved goodbye from the front door in Penywern Road. It
had been George's idea to start at night, for it meant that the worst
part of the journey would be in the cool and the dark; he had tried
it before, he told me, and found it worked.

We pedalled steadily along the Great West Road, traffic lessening
as the hour grew later; by the time we neared Taplow we had the
road all to ourselves. It was a very close night and we were glad to
stop on the bridge at Maidenhead to eat our sandwiches and have a
drink of lemonade. The stretch beyond Maidenhead was tiring, for
the road was in bad condition; my wrists went quite numb with the
jolting. George's lamp kept going out, which meant frequent stops
to re-light it, until finally he ceased to bother with it and rode close
behind me. Passing through Reading a policeman spotted him and
shouted, 'Where's your light?' We put on a spurt and left trouble
behind. As we approached Newbury a grey light promised dawn.
We stopped in the deserted street. My poor legs were as stiff as
pokers. Then came a few drops of rain. We waited under a wall,
for the rain was not heavy enough to make us don our mackintosh
capes, and after a while it stopped. We peered up at the sky, which
was leaden grey. However, we decided to go on and mounted our
bicycles. We had not gone a hundred yards before the rain came
down in torrents. The dusty road turned to mud. We floundered on

for a while but had to give it
up. We crouched for shelter
under a hedge and curled up
close together for warmth. I
promptly fell asleep. I was
wakened by a passing cyclist
shouting 'Good morning!' I felt
it was anything but a good
morning, for I was shivering
with cold. Sleepily I asked
George who his friend was. He
looked at me in surprise and
said, 'What friend?' 'That man,'
I answered. All George said
was, 'You must have been
dreaming!'

By this time the rain was falling only lightly and we agreed to
push on. Stiff and cold, we mounted our cycles and pedalled along
till we came to an inn. We did not know the time, but our thoughts
turned to breakfast and we knocked on the door. There was no
reply, so we hammered. A window above opened and a tousled
head looked out: 'What do you want?' 'Breakfast,' we called in
unison. 'Breakfast!' shouted an indignant voice. 'You won't get any
breakfast here – not at this hour.' And the window was shut with a
bang. Wearily we remounted and rode on.

It was broad daylight when we reached Hungerford – most
appropriately named, we thought – and we were lucky to find a
small eating-house open. A woman served us with tea, cold ham and
stale bread and butter. Refreshed, we had to make up our minds
what to do. It was still raining, though not so heavily, and George

said, tentatively, 'We might be able to get a train from here.' He spoke what was in my mind, though I was ashamed to admit it. 'Do you think we ought to?' George's answer was, 'We've come quite a long way and I'm soaked.' I suggested tossing up, but we agreed to go to the station and ask about a train. One was due in an hour's time, we were told, and without further hesitation we decided to take it. We bought our tickets and were doing our best to dry off in the waiting-room when the sun came out. It got warmer and warmer and blue skies appeared. 'Do you think,' I said, 'we might return our tickets and ride on?' George shook his head. 'I'm much too stiff. Sitting under that hedge was a daft thing to do.' I quite

agreed and we gave in.

It was a blazing hot morning by the time we reached Bristol, and when we arrived at the Swaishs' home in Redland Road we were almost dry and feeling more cheerful. After a late and very welcome breakfast we spent some time cleaning and oiling our cycles and then were glad to relax on deck-chairs in their garden.

George's father, a city councillor and magistrate, was the owner of several shops in the town, and his elder son Ernest was in charge of them. I had never been in Bristol and was anxious to see the town, so, later in the day, we went to have a look at the cathedral, then to the Art Gallery and ended up at the Bristol Savages Club, of which George was a member. On another occasion George took me to St

Mary Redcliffe, which I found far more interesting than the cathedral. One of the things which particularly pleased me was the famous brass lectern which was reputedly made from a life-time's collection of brass pins.

On Sunday morning I went with the family to the Baptist Chapel. I was glad to go as I had never been to a Nonconformist Chapel. I don't know what my grandfather would have thought, but I enjoyed the service and was very much impressed by the heartiness with which all joined in. George and I had often had arguments about the different forms of religious observance, for I had been brought up to regard Nonconformity with suspicion. His brother Ernest held very strong views about the hierarchy of the Church of England and a rather exaggerated view of the attitude adopted by some of the bishops. I was inclined to think that he was right. We sat and argued about it all that evening until Mrs Swaish came in and sent us off to bed.

I spent six days at Bristol and left there reluctantly to return to London and get on with my painting.

This time I cycled all the way. Starting after breakfast, I reached Chelsea late in the evening, tired and hungry, I had a meal at the 'Bug and Gluepot' and tumbled into bed.

There was still a lot of work to be done on my Tower Bridge painting, so the following evening I carried my canvas along to the wharf. Dan was sitting outside. 'I wondered if you'd be coming back,' he said. 'There's been more trouble, but they caught two of 'em at it the other night, and that's put the rest off.' Anyway, there were no more disturbances while I worked there. It was only for a few evenings, for I soon realized I could do little more to my picture on the spot. I said goodbye to Dan and carried all my things back to the studio.

But there, by myself in the evening, I could not settle to anything but wandered around feeling painfully alone in the empty studio, dissatisfied with my work and utterly depressed. I sat there long after it was dark, thinking, thinking about Florence, and hardly daring to own to myself how much I cared for her. There was no one I could talk to, for Father and Ethel had shut up the house at Blackheath and gone to Kingswear for a month. They had taken Harry Rogers' house, 'The Warren', on the cliff opposite Coombeside. I knew that Cyril was going to spend his holiday with them and the following morning I had a pleasant surprise, a letter from him. He wrote in raptures about the place and urged me to join the family there. I made up my mind to go at once and, packing my bag, I was off to Devonshire by the next train.

Cyril met me at Kingswear station and we carried my bag between us. He was full of praise for the place and spoke of his joy at seeing Gussie again. We called at Coombeside on the way. Gussie's first remark to me was: 'Why, Grandpa, what's the matter? You seem to be all eyes.' I tried to pass it off, but I was beginning to realize that I was in love. I had often been in love in a mild way before, but this was quite different and gave me no peace. It seemed so hopeless for me to think of winning Florence. I spent hours going over in my mind the times we had spent together and I could find little encouragement in anything she had said or done. There were some small crumbs of comfort here and there. I remembered how pleased she had always seemed to see me. I had told no one of my feelings, but it had taken Gussie only a few moments to realize there was something wrong with me. The next morning we started out to shop in Kingswear and, stopping at Coombeside on the way, Gussie made some excuse to call me back. I joined her in the kitchen. 'Well, Grandpa,' she said, 'I think you'd better tell me what's up.' I could

not find words to reply, so she went on: 'Come on, out with it!'
Then I told her, rather incoherently, I fear, all about Florence: how
I had known her for two years and how I had gradually grown to
love her. 'Not only is she far cleverer than I am, but she seems so
far beyond me. She must look upon me as an immature boy.
Besides,' I continued desperately,
'how many years will it be before
I can earn enough to marry, even
if she would have me?'

Gussie waited patiently while
I blundered on, then she said:
'If she loves you, she'll wait;
Groby and I had to wait ten
years.'

'It seems such cheek,' I went
on, 'that I should ever tell her that
I love her.'

Gussie flared up at this. 'Now,
Grandpa, don't talk nonsense.
No girl ever minds being told she
is loved. Where's your spirit?'

When I told her that Florence was three years older than I, her
only comment was: 'I am four years older than Groby.'

I was silent after my outpourings while Gussie went on with her
cooking. A feeling of relief came over me, relief that I had been able
to tell her and have her sympathy. Presently she came across and
kissed me. 'Don't worry, Grandpa,' she said. 'It'll turn out all right.
The sun may be shining tomorrow.'

It did not shine the next day, but it did a week later, for I had a
letter from Suffolk. It had been forwarded from Blackheath Post

Office and I hardly dared to open it. It was from Florence, asking me to stay with them at the Red House.

Dear Kipper,

If you can spare the time from your picture do come and stay with us here. You never told me how you got on in Bristol. With love from

Florence.

I tried to contain my feelings, and then, at the first opportunity, dashed across the valley to Coombeside. Gussie and Groby were in the garden. I rushed up to her, took her in my arms and kissed her. 'Um,' she said, 'Grandpa's feeling better. It must be the Devon air!' I showed her my letter. 'Well, I suppose you'll be off tomorrow,' she commented, and I was.

Gussie's last remark as we said goodbye was 'Tell Florence that if she wants a nice quiet holiday with humdrum people, adequate cooking and plenty of Devonshire cream, she is to come to Coombeside.'

'What a grand idea!' was all that I could say.

Chapter Fourteen

ENGAGED

I T was too late to travel that day so I hurried into Kingswear
and sent a telegram to Florence. Then I repacked my bag and
next morning I left. The night at the studio *en route* was much
happier than the one I had spent there the previous week. In the
morning after a hasty cup of tea I put all my things in my cycle
valise and set off for Liverpool Street Station. This part of the journey
did not take me long. Cycling in London before the advent of the
motor car was very different from what it is now. Horse-drawn
traffic moved slowly and drivers would signal with their whips
before stopping or making a turn. Fast-trotting hansoms and tradesmen's gigs were hazards, as were the barrows of itinerant vendors
moving along by the kerb, but traffic blocks were almost unknown,
and at only a few busy corners in the City and West End were policemen stationed to take control.

I had no idea what time there would be a train to Saxmundham,
and when I reached the station I found I had a long time to wait,
so I had a meal. Eventually I reached Saxmundham at four o'clock
and half an hour later was at the Red House at Hinton.

All the family were gathered at the farm next door to celebrate
the arrival of a litter of pigs and I was greeted with excited shouts
but was not allowed to see the piglings. There were a lot of people
at tea, various neighbours having dropped in; I was very pleased to

To celebrate the arrival of a litter of pigs

be treated almost as one of the family. They made me tell Mrs Chaplin of my experiences painting in dockland. She was a very handsome woman who had been a widow for several years. Her husband 'Jimmy' Chaplin had been a member of Lloyd's and, among other things, had had a nice taste in old furniture and a keen appreciation of the arts; he had counted a number of artists among his friends.

So Florence had been brought up in a congenial atmosphere, something like mine.

After supper I was shown the Family Album. There were all the Chaplin children, five girls and three boys. There was a picture of Florence aged four, very fat and smug, with dark curls, and another, taken at the seaside, of the three younger girls in jersey frocks. A later picture showed the girls when they were at school at Spa in Belgium. There was a daguerreotype of Ebenezer Landells, one of the founders of *Punch*, who was Mrs Chaplin's father, and another of her brother Robert, also an artist and one who had served as War Correspondent to *The Illustrated London News* during the Franco-Prussian War of 1870.

After breakfast next morning there was some talk of going in a party to Southwold, but Florence's sisters were quick to realize that she and I might like to be on our own, and they started for Southwold alone. Florence and I set off on our bicycles in the opposite direction with the intention of visiting Blythburgh. The country was a complete contrast to Devon – flat, with a wide horizon. Presently our attention wandered from the landscape. I told Florence about my stay at Kingswear and how delighted I had been to receive her letter. Thinking we had found a short cut, we followed a sandy track, but this soon petered out and we realized we had lost our way. It was rough common land and the only living thing in sight was a tethered donkey who, after regarding us for a few minutes, resumed his feeding and took no further interest in us.

Florence asked me how I got my nickname. I told her I had earned it at the age of sixteen while a student at Heatherley's. 'Arthur Connor and Chattie Wake and – ' I said. She stopped me. 'Why Chattie and I were friends at the Royal College of Art! We both started our training there. I remember her lovely mane of red hair. She left when I did and I haven't seen her since.' I told her that Chattie left Heatherley's to go to Rolshoven's School, and though I had not seen her for two years we still wrote to each other.

After a pause Florence said: 'I think "Kip" suits you.' And she went on: 'I have a nickname, too. It sounds rather a silly one – "Pie". I have had it since I was four years old. It was given me by my father as a kind of joke. You saw from that photo in the album how fat I was as a child. He used to chaff me about this, and make me kneel before him and say: "Pity the poor starving skelington!" I did not know what this meant, but it always provoked peals of laughter. Then he would say: "What would the poor thing like to eat?" and I always answered "Pie, please! Pie, please! Pie, please!" '

Quickly I said: 'Then I shall call you "Pie".'

'Yes, do! I like it much better than Florence, and Florrie is just awful.'

We sat on and she asked me about my boyhood. I told her of

our happy childhood before Mother's death, about the Aunts and Lizzie, and our meeting with Gussie again. 'I have a message from Gussie for you,' I said.

'For me!' She looked surprised. 'Whatever can it be?'

'It is to go and see them in Devonshire.'

'But –' she hesitated.

I went on: 'I told Gussie – I *had* to tell her, for she guessed at once – I was in love with you. I didn't think I ought to tell you, but she said I should and that you wouldn't mind.'

I waited, not daring to look at her.

Then I said: 'Do tell me you don't mind.'

'Of course I don't, Kip. I love you, but I don't know whether I do like that.' She sat quite still, and when I looked at her I saw tears in her eyes.

'Oh, Pie!' I burst out. 'I can't bear to worry you or make you unhappy, but I do love you so much and will try never to spoil things for you.' I had a haunting fear that there might be someone else, it seemed impossible that there should not be. But I knew that I must say no more then.

After a while I went back to talking of just ordinary things – like my working down at the docks; my life with George at the studio; our cheap meals in the Brompton Road . . . Then I asked her to tell me about herself.

'It isn't very exciting,' she said.

'But you showed me some photos of Belgium last night. Do tell me about that.'

'Connie and Addie and I went to a school at Spa kept by a Madame Lecocq. We were the only English girls; the others were all German or Belgian. We had much more freedom than at an English school. I was there three years. We all learned to speak

French fluently and were very happy. We still keep up with Madame by writing. The German girls were sometimes rather a trial; they were inclined to panic on the slightest provocation. One evening we were all in the schoolroom doing our prep when we heard a scream. A German girl had been sent upstairs to fetch something and she burst in gasping, *"Ein Mann! Ein Mann!"* We all went upstairs in a body and found a dummy sitting on a chair in the dormitory. Two of the Belgians were responsible for rigging it up. We never let the Germans forget it . . .! *"Ein Mann!"* we would call out whenever anything unusual happened.'

I told Pie about our trip to Germany and how we stopped the waterfall near the Brocken. We were both laughing when the time came to cycle home.

When we reached the Red House, Pie went in but was out again almost immediately. 'I wanted to make sure the boys were out,' she said. Then: 'Come and look here!' She led me across the garden and stopped by a fruit tree laden with what appeared to be green plums. She picked several and handed me some. 'The boys think they are plums and are waiting impatiently for them to ripen. They are really greengages. Aren't they delicious?' I readily agreed they were. Then Pie went on: 'Addie discovered this last week and we have to be careful; if the boys see us eating them they'd finish the lot in no time.' The 'boys' were Pie's younger brother Lindsay and his cousin Percy who was staying in the house. It was not long

before the secret was out. Pie's sister was caught in the act of picking. The boys were furious and our behaviour was described as 'caddish'!

One afternoon we cycled to Walberswick – 'Wobbleswick' as Charles Keene called it. I knew that he had often been there and I recognized the backgrounds of many of his lovely drawings. Pie admired his work as much as I did. I still have the etching, given me by Keene's brother many years later, of the old wooden jetty. I was so happy to be with Pie and to know that she liked being with me. There was always the hope that some day she might care for me as much as I did for her. But then would come the depressing thought:

'How long will it be before I can earn enough to ask her to marry me?' Well, for the time being I should see her at the Schools, though not for long, for her time as a student was nearly up. The prospect of losing her, however, was avoided by her decision to share a studio in the Fulham Road with a friend.

My Landseer Scholarship had now expired, and I was no longer compelled to work every day at the Schools. I spent more time at Glebe Place making black-and-white drawings. Then I received a commission to illustrate *Tom Brown's Schooldays*. I had a copy of the original edition (my prize won at 'Bewsher's') with the fine illustrations by Arthur Hughes and Sydney P. Hall, and I found it difficult to avoid being unduly influenced by them.

I was able to see Pie at her studio and went there as often as possible, but owing to the state of Father's health I had to spend more and more time at Blackheath. An operation he had recently undergone, though slight enough in itself, had affected his arthritis and he could now hardly walk.

Part of my time at Blackheath was spent in looking for subjects to paint and I found some in Morden College. The little chapel appealed to me particularly and I promised myself I would paint it when circumstances permitted. These preoccupations meant that I could not see Pie as often as I wished, but I was comforted by the feeling that she was growing fonder of me; I was sure, at least, that I was very much in her confidence, and I knew I was able to help her in a number of ways.

Early that spring she was commissioned to carry out her prize mural design in the nurses' dining-hall at Guy's Hospital. It was a big undertaking and she decided to do the work in oils. The huge canvas was prepared – twenty-five feet long – and fixed to the wall. As the painting was high up a movable platform on wheels was

made. I went with her to see it set up. The canvas looked very big and rather frightening, but we had fun climbing up on the platform and starting to square it out. In March she came two or three times to Blackheath after working all the morning at the mural; it was easy to take a train from London Bridge. I had painted a water-colour in our garden, and she stood for me where the daffodils were coming into bloom. I called the picture 'The Eve of April'.

Father was very pleased when she came, for he knew how much I loved her and I think he hoped we might become engaged. He was growing more and more crippled and his doctor advised us to consult a specialist. The consultation took place in London, and after the examination we were told that Father was suffering from disseminated sclerosis and that there was no chance of his getting better. We must prepare ourselves for the gradual loss of control of all his limbs. This was a great shock. When we reached home Ethel, Cyril and I sat down to talk things over. We should probably need the services of a male nurse – someone strong who could lift Father. We should also need to hire a wheel-chair. The trouble was that we did not know Father's financial position. When we did find it out we were shocked. Father, always an optimist, felt sure that he could be cured by a sea-voyage, and I said I would go with him if the money were forthcoming. Of course it was not; and we arranged instead to take him to Dover for a week. He had the happiest memories of the place as he and Mother had spent part of their honeymoon there. We booked rooms in an old house on the sea-front and took him by train. He could just walk the few steps to the carriage. We hired a wheel-chair in the town, and though the weather was cold and stormy he liked to go out. We pushed his chair along the sea-front, struggling against the boisterous winds. Cyril came down for the week-end and at the end of the time we managed between us to get Father home. It was the last time he was to leave our house at Blackheath.

Back at home again our doctor found us a male nurse, a retired Irish Guardsman, a great big fellow called Howse, who was more than equal to Father's weight and who lifted him into his chair and took him for airings on the Heath. Soon Father became too feeble to go out. Old friends, including Frank and Minnie Dicksee, came to see him. His mind was perfectly clear till near the end, but he was quite helpless. Our dear old Lizzie, who had been with us for years, was heartbroken. I gave up going to town, and Ethel, Cyril and I took it in turns to sit up with Father at night. Towards the end of April Aunt Fanny came and took her share of the watching. Early in May Father died. He was only fifty-six.

The illness had cost a lot of money and there was hardly anything left. Cyril and I had a difficult interview with the bank manager, who pointed out that our best course – in fact our only course – was to sell the lease of our house. We were spared one anxiety: Lizzie's future. She told us that we need not worry about her as she and her sisters had inherited a considerable sum of money from a distant

188

relative. It appeared that the old gentleman, about whom she had sometimes spoken, had made a fortune in the City. So the three old ladies bought a house in Streatham (and a piano) and spent their declining years in peace and comfort.

We sold our house, stored most of our furniture and moved into rooms in Hyde Vale, close to the Heath. I told George that I could no longer afford the studio and he readily agreed to take over for the last few months till our agreement terminated. I was able to start my painting in the Chapel at Morden College. I answered an advertisement for a 'tame' artist to work in a newspaper office, but this proved to be a whole-time job, and as the pay was only two pounds a week I did not think it good enough.

Though we had been poor for so many years, until now it had never seemed to matter. Living among fellow students, all as impecunious as myself, being 'hard-up' was the normal condition. One did not look ahead or make plans for the future. Now everything was different, and I must think of someone besides myself. I had come to realize how much I relied on Pie's sympathy and understanding and that I was, in fact, in danger of taking too much for granted. She fully understood how I felt about Father's death, for she had lost her own father only five years before and this had obliged her family to cut down all expenses and to take in paying guests in order to keep the house going. She had a far clearer view of the things that matter in life than I had, and, sitting beside me on the sofa in her studio, she rallied me for being so downhearted.

'I can't help worrying,' I said, 'for the one thing in life that I long for seems so far away. I am longing to marry you, but how can I ask you when I have absolutely nothing to offer you?'

She said: 'I suppose money is important.' Then she went on: 'You might sell your picture.'

I shook my head. 'It's no good relying on that. I must tout round and get more black-and-white work.'

She broke in: 'I shall have a hundred pounds when I have finished my mural.'

'But, Pie, that's *yours*! I should never dream . . .'

She cut me short: 'Surely it's a much better way for us to share everything. But –' Here she smiled at me. 'You haven't yet asked me to marry you, have you?'

'Oh, Pie, darling . . . I . . . Will you?'

She just answered: 'Yes, Kip.'

I was so overcome I couldn't speak. I took her two hands in mine, she put her head on my shoulder and we sat there close together, holding each other, like a couple of children.

Chapter Fifteen

FINDING A COTTAGE

I WENT back to our dim lodgings in Hyde Vale that evening feeling as if the heavens had opened and bestowed a benediction on me. Ethel and Cyril were delighted when I told them. Ethel was writing a letter to Gussie telling her of the change in our fortunes and I asked her to add my good news and say I would write myself in a day or two.

Cyril and I slept together at the top of the house; our room was overcrowded with furniture, for we had kept back as much as possible to save the cost of storage. We lay in bed and talked far into the night. He agreed that the best plan was for Pie and me to find a cottage in the country, not too far from London, where we could live really cheaply. We could not be married for at least a year; that is to say, until Pie had finished her mural at Guy's Hospital. Meanwhile I must work as hard as I could. In some trepidation I wrote to my two surviving aunts. I had not seen Aunt Ellen for three years. She had left Steyning and now lived at Watford. Since Aunt Alicia's death and the sale of the big house in Gordon Square, Aunt Fanny had lived in a small house in Woburn Place near St Pancras Church, with the faithful Jane in attendance.

I knew that I must face Pie's mother, who would naturally want to know about my prospects, and I put off the interview as long as possible until Pie said I must face it. 'I don't think you need worry,' she said. 'Mother is fond of you and is quite used to having very little money herself.' So I went the next day. I think Mrs Chaplin disliked talking about money matters as much as I did, for she did not ask me if I had a settled income, or what it was. I said I was prepared to take on any work and that we hoped to be able to live quite cheaply. She said, 'There is one thing I insist on. You must insure your life.' I readily agreed; and that was about all that was said on the subject of money. We then talked of our future prospects and of my plan to find a cottage in the country. She said: 'I cannot give Florence any allowance, but I will give her some furniture when you find your cottage.' She went on to tell me she was giving up her house in Penywern Road and moving to Deal and was sure she would have some to spare. I was very grateful to her, for I was afraid she might insist on our waiting until I was earning a steady income.

I did not have to wait long for a letter from Aunt Fanny. She wrote: 'This *is* a surprise and I hope you will be very happy. You must bring Miss Chaplin to see me.' Pie had heard so much about my aunts that she was rather shy about accepting the invitation, but she summoned up her courage, put on her best dress and, wearing a new hat, joined me at Earls Court Station and we took the Underground to Gower Street. Aunt Fanny had invited us to tea and was sitting in

the drawing-room with the table ready laid when we arrived. As we went in she rose and came forward to meet Pie. Taking both Pie's hands, she smilingly said: 'My niece!' Then looking steadily at Pie for a moment she kissed her. It was done so simply and sweetly. We sat down and told her of our plans. She showed no concern over the risks we were prepared to take and seemed to have perfect faith in my ability to earn a living. She said: 'I got quite cross with your Uncle Willie. When I told him about your engagement he was horrified and said you should not dream of getting married until you had a sufficient income. I said "Stuff and nonsense! They're old enough to know what they are about."' I could feel Pie's heart warming towards my dear little aunt.

Aunt Ellen reacted a little differently. She showed some bewilderment at our rashness, but she added: 'I have lived alone and been out of touch with modern life for so long that I find it difficult to understand how you can both be brave enough to marry with such slender prospects. But, my dear boy, you have my warmest blessing. Please bring Miss Chaplin to see me if she can forgive a very deaf old lady.'

After hearing what Aunt Fanny had told me I was not surprised to receive a letter from Uncle Willie. He said he was rather shocked to hear that I contemplated marriage at such an early age (I was twenty-four) and with no settled income. He himself, when a young master at St Paul's School, had married and found it difficult to make ends meet, even though he had private means to supplement his salary. He begged me to consider the matter most carefully before I embarked on such a course.

We *had* considered the matter most carefully. One evening after dinner at Roche's we had sat at our corner table and totted up what we would have to spend on rent, food and coal. We had quite agreed that a cottage should be our home, and after Pie had assured

me that she would love to
live in the country, she said:
'I have enough clothes to last
me for ages, and it will be
fun trying to cook.'

I think it cannot have been
easy for anyone brought up as
Uncle Willie had been to
understand the courage of a
girl who was prepared to
share the life of a penniless
artist. I was earning something
with my black-and-white
drawings, though my efforts to get a drawing accepted by *Punch*
were fruitless: it was two years before I achieved that.

I spent part of every day working on my picture in the chapel
at Morden College. I was determined to finish it in time to send it
to next year's Academy. Whenever I could I went to Guy's Hospital
to give Pie a hand. There was a narrow border to her mural, a
repetitive design that was tiresome to paint, and I was able to work
on this, doing a yard at a time, while she worked on her figures.
It was a constant joy to me to watch her paint, for she was so sure
and direct and rarely had to repaint anything. As the work progressed, so the scaffold had to be constantly shifted. The nurses
helped Pie with this unless I was there, when we would manage it
between us.

Gussie's reply to my letter was prompt and characteristic. After
expressing her joy at our engagement she wrote: 'You must bring
Florence to stay with us and I would like to ask Ethel and Cyril too.
I am sure you all need a rest after the trouble you have been through.

L'ART NOUVEAU

Painting the mural—a contemporary sketch

I cannot ask you all to stay here, the house is not large enough, but I could have Florence and could get rooms at the farm for you three. Let me know when Cyril has his holiday and I will see what I can do.' This was a wonderful invitation, and when I told Pie she said she would be glad to have a fortnight off from her painting. Ethel, Cyril and I put our heads together over the cost and agreed to pool our resources for a fortnight in August when Cyril's leave was due. It was rash of us to spend the money, but the pleasure of looking forward and afterwards of looking back was compensation enough.

Neither George nor Arthur betrayed surprise when I told them of my engagement. 'This is a family affair,' said George, 'and I hope you'll ask us to your wedding.'

'No doubt about that,' I said, and went on to tell them of our plans to find a cottage in the country. Arthur was concerned about our sketchy finances; living at home, as he was, and in receipt of an allowance, the spirit of adventure did not appeal to him. 'Who will do your cooking?' he asked.

'Ourselves, of course,' I said. 'I can make excellent porridge and can grill chops, and Pie is learning to cook. We shall manage and we'll invite you to a meal when we are settled in.'

Arthur looked a bit dubious about this, then he said: 'Look, I am going to paint a portrait of a cousin of mine in Surrey in June or July, and if you like I will make inquiries round about. My cousins live in Shamley Green, a village near Guildford, and I shall stay in rooms in Albury, where I have been before. There may be something in that neighbourhood.'

George suggested that it would be nice if we came near Bristol, but I explained that that was too far from London.

A few weeks later I heard from Arthur. The letter was written from Albury and asked me to join him there. He said his cousin Mrs Nelson knew of a cottage on the Cranleigh Road that was vacant. He could give me no details of the place except that it belonged to a Mrs Arbuthnot. I packed a few clothes and was off on my cycle.

Arthur's cousins lived at 'Long Acre', a house by Shamley Green. Sir Charles Crosthwaite, whose portrait he was painting, had been Governor of the North-West Province of India, and Mrs Nelson was his daughter. I found her a charming lady and most sympathetic. 'The cottage,' she said, 'is very small and has been empty for some time. I have no idea whether Mrs Arbuthnot is prepared to let it, but there is no harm in finding out.' She told me where it was and I went off to investigate.

I came to the cross-roads at Stroud Common and asked at a tiny shop on the corner. A little woman in a black straw hat came from a back room. After I had bought a packet of cigarettes for fourpence, she was quite ready to tell me all she knew about the cottage. Then

she said: 'You'd best go down the
road to Upper House and ask the
gardener there. His name is Foxall
and he has the key.' I pedalled down
the road and came to Upper House.
It had a long drive with stables on
the right-hand side. There was a
lad cutting grass with a fag-hook
and I asked him for Mr Foxall and
was directed to the garden. Mr
Foxall said that the cottage had been
empty for over a year and needed 'a

bit of doing up'. It might be to let, but he couldn't say. I had best
write to Mrs Arbuthnot. He gave me her address in London and
then we walked up the road to see the place.

I was not impressed. It was very small and square with a porch
in front and no architectural pretensions. The roof was of slate and
the overgrown garden had a railing with a gate on to the road.
Foxall produced a key and we went in. The kitchen, on the left, had
a brick floor, a decent-looking range, and a box staircase leading
upstairs. A sitting-room on the right smelt of damp and the paper
was peeling off the walls. There was a scullery with a pump at the
back and a sort of larder beyond. Upstairs were two bedrooms with
fireplaces and a tiny room under the eaves behind. The windows
were iron framed with leaded lights. 'There's no water, you know,'
said Foxall. 'There's a well, but I wouldn't drink the water, it's
mostly surface drainage.' My heart was sinking rapidly as I asked
about the sanitary arrangements. 'Oh, that!' said Foxall. 'It's out
in that shed.' Then he added: 'You can always draw water from
Mrs Wilson at the corner, they have a good well there that never

runs dry.' I kept wondering whether Pie could endure such primitive conditions. There was quite a stretch of garden at the back with two or three apple-trees and a blackberry hedge.

I asked Foxall about the rent. He said: 'Maybe you could have it for seven and sixpence a week, but I can't say – you must write to Mrs Arbuthnot.' He became quite communicative as we walked back to Upper House. He told me

he had been Lily Langtry's gardener for years and found his present job mighty dull. As I left him he said: 'Mind you, I can give you no promise, but I expect the old lady will be glad to have the place occupied.'

I mounted my bicycle and pedalled about for miles to think things over. I climbed Ewhurst Hill and at the top saw a 'notice 'To Let' on a small house. Behind it was a larger house with a drive. I went along this and found the front door ajar. I knocked and pushed it open. A rumbling voice inside called: 'Who is it?' 'I am looking for a house,' I replied, 'and I see you have one to let.' 'Come in,' said the voice. I went in and found myself in a large studio. An old man was seated in an armchair in a corner wearing a dark-blue cloak draped over his shoulders and a skull-cap. There were several large canvases on easels and the room smelt of oil paint and tobacco smoke. I asked about the house to let. The rent, he told me, was £50 a year.

I thanked him and retreated. As I left he said: 'If you think of taking it, write to me. My name is Clayton Adams.' I realized that however much I might admire his landscapes I could not afford his rent.

I returned home the following day and wrote a letter to Mrs Arbuthnot telling her that I had seen her cottage and asking her if she were willing to let it. The reply she sent me was not encouraging. She said: 'I don't know what that man Foxall told you, but he has no right to make any arrangements. I have not made any plans at present about letting the cottage, as I may want it for one of my staff.'

I showed the letter to Pie and we agreed that this was not a definite refusal. The phrase 'at present' held out some hope and I said that I would return to the attack later. I had no time to go exploring again, and though I wrote to house agents in Guildford and Cranleigh the 'To Lets' they sent me were too expensive.

Pie and I were having dinner at our corner table at Roche's when I told her about the cottage. I drew her a picture of it with a plan of the rooms. She did not seem alarmed about the drinking-water or the lack of modern conveniences, but was worried about baths. 'I have got a hip bath that belonged to my aunts,' I observed tentatively. 'But we should have to heat the water for it on the kitchen range.' Pie thought this would be rather fun and was delighted at the prospect of a garden with apple-trees. 'There would be nowhere to paint,' I said, and we agreed that we must have a studio of some kind put up in the garden as soon as we could afford it.

Ethel, Cyril and I were in high spirits when we met Pie at Paddington Station for our holiday in Devon. On the journey we discussed the housing problem, toying with the idea of looking for something in Devon, but I knew that however alluring the prospect, it would not work; we had to find something nearer London. We travelled via Bath and Bristol and I was happy to point out to Pie all the landmarks on my beloved Great Western Railway. As we came in sight of the Dart, with *Britannia* and *Hindustan* anchored in the river, we leaned from our carriage window and sang like children on a school treat! Gussie, Groby and Snap were waiting on the platform at Kingswear Station and we all crowded into a wagonette and drove off, stopping at Green Park Farm where Cyril, Ethel and I were to stay. The farm was only half a mile across the fields from Coombeside, and after putting us down with our luggage the wagonette drove on with Gussie, Groby and Pie; Gussie calling back to us: 'Come along for tea. It will be ready in half an hour.' Green Park Farm was pleasantly situated with great 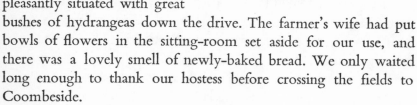 bushes of hydrangeas down the drive. The farmer's wife had put bowls of flowers in the sitting-room set aside for our use, and there was a lovely smell of newly-baked bread. We only waited long enough to thank our hostess before crossing the fields to Coombeside.

I was not a bit surprised to find Pie already perfectly at home. She was brimming over with excitement and eager to explore the valley. We did this after tea, climbing the path up to The Warren. We looked in through the windows and saw Harry Rogers' organ, now nearly completed and quite filling the room. Harry and Herbert were away on their annual trip to the moors and had left a message for us giving us the free use of their boat. We took them at their word and were out most days in search of mackerel. These were very scarce, but we had one good afternoon and took the catch to Coombeside, where Pie helped Gussie to cook a glorious supper.

It was a lovely holiday, and like all lovely holidays the days of it passed swiftly by. The last evening was spent at Coombeside, Groby producing a bottle of old liqueur brandy for the occasion. I had tasted brandy in France but nothing like this vintage. We all drank a toast to 'Health, Wealth and Happiness'.

Chapter Sixteen

OUR GREAT ADVENTURE

BOTH Pie and I had a lot of hard work ahead of us but our holiday had done us so much good that we were able to tackle it with renewed vigour. The mural was going well, almost half of it being finished. But as the days drew in Pie was not able to give so much time to it. Since her mother gave up the house in Earls Court she had been living with her sister Connie at Norbury. Connie was married to Henry Young, a doctor practising in Norbury and Streatham; their house was near the station, but the journey to Guy's Hospital was tedious and there were many days in winter when the light was too bad for work in the dining-hall. I had to give up painting in the chapel, partly for the same reason and partly also because the place was not warmed and was like an icehouse in the cold weather. I filled in my time with black-and-white work and was commissioned to illustrate two books.

Both were very dull. One was a story about the earthquake in Martinique and bore the title *Smouldering Fires*. I cannot think why the publishers should have chosen me as the illustrator, for I knew nothing about the place and had to spend a lot of time trying to find out. However, these small jobs brought in ten or fifteen pounds, so I was able to put something by.

The cottage was constantly in my mind, but I was too much occupied to do anything about it then. Later on I would try and get a definite answer from Mrs Arbuthnot.

I was glad when the spring came and I could finish my work in the chapel. I was not very satisfied with the result, but I bought a frame for four pounds and was somewhat reassured when I showed my work to George and Arthur, for George said: 'It's jolly well painted.' Sending-in day at the Royal Academy was at the end of March and I carried my picture to Burlington House wrapped in a dust-sheet. The thing looked very insignificant among the large and important canvases stacked in the corridor and I offered up a silent prayer as I came away. Outside in the yard the students were lounging on the bench. I did not see any familiar faces. It seemed an age since I myself had sat there with my friends. I pushed open the swing door

leading to the Schools and found Osborne, the porter, in his office. He grumbled about the present-day students. 'Not the same as in your day,' he said. I fancy he may have been saying the same thing to every past student for twenty years or more. Then I went to Guy's Hospital to see Pie and forget all about my picture.

The mural was nearing completion. She was working on the central group, which included the figure of a small winged boy. Presently the nurses trooped in to their luncheon; they stood looking up and one of them asked: 'How much longer will it take?' She went on: 'We all think it is lovely and will be sorry when it's finished. We have enjoyed watching you paint so much.' Pie told me that she had heard from Sir Cooper Perry, the doctor who was responsible for commissioning the work, that an additional £50 was to be given her for her expenses. She was in high glee and said: 'I have reckoned it up and find that it has not cost me that, so we shall have something over.'

Three weeks after sending-in day I heard from the Academy that my picture was accepted and a varnishing ticket followed. Varnishing day was a great occasion, when artists were able to see their accepted pictures in the galleries – the lucky ones hung on the line. Some of the less fortunate, whose pictures were 'skied', could be seen on ladders touching up their work, piling on the colour to bring the pictures to notice; one in particular, I remember, was splashing on scarlet paint. I was one of the lucky ones, for my picture was on the line in the second room. I met several friends and one of them told me that Edwin Abbey was in one of the galleries. I promptly went in search of him and found him deep in

conversation with a fellow Royal Academician. I waited till presently he saw me and greeted me with: 'Hallo, Shepard, what are you doing here?' I told him and he went on: 'You should go on with your black and white, you know. Have you tried *Punch*?' I told him of my unsuccessful efforts. 'You must meet Linley Sambourne,' he said. 'He's somewhere about. Come along and I'll introduce you.' He took my arm and we charged from room to room.

Sambourne was talking to a friend. He was the senior cartoonist for *Punch*, having taken John Tenniel's place three years earlier. He turned towards us while Abbey, holding my arm, said: 'Here, Sambourne, do you know Shepard? A promising young artist who wants to get into *Punch*.' Then he gave me a dig as though to say, 'Now get on with it,' and left us. I stammered a few words in praise of Sambourne's work, but he cut me short and talked about *Punch*. He said: 'You want to get hold of some good jokes, make rough sketches and fire them in.' I told him of my failures. 'Of course,' he said; 'that happens to everyone. You've got to go on. Give them no peace!' He left me feeling rather bewildered. I went out to get some lunch and on my return met a student friend on the stairs. He told me Frank Dicksee was looking for me.

Frank was very tall and always wore a frock-coat, so he was easily found. 'I like your picture,' he said, 'but there is no price on it. Is it for sale?' 'Oh yes,' I answered. Frank went on: 'Hamo Thornycroft and I have been deputed to buy a picture for a colonial art gallery and we both would like to buy yours. We can only spend £100 – can you sell it for that?' My voice, I fear, was hardly audible. 'Yes,' I said, 'I shall be very glad to. Thank you so much.' Frank then said: 'I expect you'll find the money useful when you get married.' I was able to answer heartily, 'Indeed we shall!' A hundred pounds was more than I should have dared to ask. I had thought of sixty guineas, but George had advised me not to price the picture; an experienced artist had told him to wait until one's picture was hung before fixing the price. I was thankful I had followed his advice. Now the whole situation was changed and I could go ahead with the cottage. I sent a telegram to Pie, who was staying at Deal with her mother. She told me afterwards it was almost unintelligible and read as if I had made some money in a colonial investment.

When I reached home that evening I wrote to Mrs Arbuthnot. As I concocted my letter I prayed that the place was still vacant. I had to wait a month for a reply. 'I have been abroad,' she said. 'If you want to rent my cottage you had better come and see me about it.' I seized on this ray of hope and wrote asking for an appointment. Her reply a week later was written in the third person and named a day and hour at which I was to present myself at her house in Mayfair. When the day came I made my way to South Street, found the house and rang the bell. The door was opened by a maid; as I paused on the door-step and asked for my hostess, a voice from somewhere inside said: 'Wipe your feet!' I wiped my feet and passing in was shown into a sitting-room. The owner of the voice was standing by the window. She was tall and stout and wore a large hat. 'Why do you want my cottage?' she asked. I explained I was marrying a wife and wanted somewhere to live. 'It's not the kind of place *I* would want to live in,' she went on. 'I don't want to have any bother with it. If I let it you must do it up and keep it in repair, and be prepared to turn out if I want it.' This struck me as a rather one-sided arrangement, and I said I hoped she would give me at least a year's tenancy with the option of staying on. Her reply was: 'I don't want to be bothered with it, I must think it over.' I explained that I would be glad to have a definite answer as I wanted to marry in the autumn and time would be needed to do the place up. I asked her if she would take this into consideration and let me know the rent. 'Oh, the rent!' she said. 'I should not charge much – perhaps half a crown a week.' I thanked her and asked her if she would give me permission to take possession of the cottage. She replied: 'I will write a form of agreement. We need not go to the expense of a lawyer.' That ended the interview and I came away satisfied with the rent she named, but not easy in my mind about my position. Could I go ahead and make plans with a builder to have the place done up on so vague a promise? I consulted Cyril and he advised me to chance it. When Pie came back to London to her sister's house we talked it over together; she agreed with me and was all for going ahead. So I packed my valise and cycled to Shamley Green.

The cottage looked much the same, the weeds perhaps even more in evidence. I went to Upper House and routed out Foxall, telling him that I had taken the cottage. I said that an agreement was being drawn up and I had been promised the place for a year. Meanwhile I should like the key so that I could make plans with a builder for repairs. Foxall demurred. He had had no word from Mrs Arbuthnot and could not hand over the place like that. 'She might change her mind,' he said. 'She's done it before.' I refused to be put off and offered to take entire responsibility for anything that might happen. He relented at this and went so far as to tell me of a builder on the Cranleigh Road, a small firm that might be willing to do the job. I went off and found the builder's yard quite easily. A workman told me to come back in an hour as the builder was out. I cycled on to Cranleigh and had a look round and booked myself a room for the night at an inn. The builder was there when I reached the yard again and he agreed to go with me to see the cottage and give an estimate, but warned me it would be a month before he could start work. He had a trap waiting outside, so we drove in that with my bicycle tied on the back. He spent a long time going from room to room, tapping the walls and testing the woodwork with a penknife. He lit paper in the fireplaces and shook his head over the damp patches in the sitting-room. He said that if the walls were treated I might have a nice bit of panelling fixed as a dado, but I said that papering the walls would satisfy me. He went outside, fetched his ladder from the trap and had a look at the roof. 'Sound enough on the outside,' was

his comment, but short of removing the
slates there was no means of inspecting
the timbers. He condemned the system
of drainage. He stood looking at the gully
by the back door and picked up a bit of
stick and poked about among the dead
leaves. 'You'll have trouble with that,' he
said. 'There ain't enough fall.' He was
right. We did have trouble, endless
trouble, with that gully. Finally he agreed
to post me an estimate within a few days.

When I reached home a letter awaited
me from Mrs Arbuthnot, enclosing a
form of agreement drawn up on a sheet of
writing paper. It was a strange document;
I don't know what a house agent would
have said about it. It stated simply: 'Mrs
Arbuthnot is prepared to let her cottage
to Mr Shepard for one year certain on condition that he does it up
thoroughly and keeps it in repair.' The accompanying note directed
me to affix a sixpenny stamp, sign the document and return it
to the sender. Though I was no business man it seemed to me
that there were some things lacking in this, but I was ready to
take a chance. The rent at least was modest – even more modest, I
decided after much calculation, than the 2s. 6d. a week Mrs Arbuthnot had suggested when I called on her: £6 a year works out at
2s. 3½d. a week. The difference of 10s. was more than enough to pay
for the stamp.

I carried the agreement with me when I went to report progress
to Pie. I had arranged to meet her at Guy's Hospital and help her

pack up her painting things. The mural was finished and at last we could see the whole thing unobstructed by the scaffolding. It looked grand, and Pie flushed with pleasure as several nurses and students

congratulated her. One of the students gave her a bunch of flowers. I went back to Norbury with her and told of the builder's verdict on our cottage and that work could not start before September so that our wedding would have to wait till the end of the month. We talked it over with Connie and her husband and had a good laugh over my 'Agreement'. The Youngs had already offered to lend their house for our wedding reception and suggested that we should be married in their parish church. This would solve a problem, for Mrs Chaplin was living at Deal and we did not want to be married there. So it was arranged, and Mrs Chaplin came to Norbury a few days later for a family conclave at which our wedding was fixed for September 28th. Already it was August, so there was not much time. I wrote to my aunts, to Uncle Willie and my near friends. Pie and I went over our lists together and chose those of our fellow students who should be invited.

I had a charming reply from Aunt Ellen, who expressed her regret that she was not able to come and enclosed a most generous cheque. Uncle Willie turned up trumps, as he always did: no longer criticizing our rashness, he wished us every form of happiness and backed it with a cheque for £25. Aunt Fannie, accepting the invitation, said that her present would be groceries from Shoolbred's. Pie had a canteen of cutlery from her uncle and aunt; the Dicksees gave me a gate-legged table; and Mrs Chaplin, besides her gift of the Suffolk Dower Press, gave us a carpet and some chairs. One of the best presents promised to us was from Annie Gregory. She had been a very close friend of my mother's, and was the wife of Charles Gregory, the painter and member of the Royal Water Colour Society. They lived at Milford in Surrey and it was outside their house when they lived in Ripley that I had disgraced myself at an early age by lying on my back in the middle of the road and screaming. She wrote offering to go to our cottage on our wedding day and prepare it for our arrival – light the fires, air the sheets and cook us a dinner. I wrote an enthusiastic acceptance of her offer with instructions where to find the key.

When the builder's estimate came in it was lower than I had expected – under £16 – so I wrote accepting it and asking for an early start with the work. Ethel and Cyril, who fully shared my excitement, volunteered to go with me and help to get the cottage ready. Cyril felt that our presence would have the effect of hurrying the builders. As he could get away only at week-ends, it was arranged that Ethel and I should pack a trunk with linen, blankets and a few stores and camp in the cottage and Cyril would join us when he could. So, a week later, Ethel and I were off. Besides our suitcases we had the trunk, a box of kitchen ware and some stores. The local 'fly' drove us from Bramley Station. We found the cottage in a rare mess, with workmen in the bedrooms distempering the ceilings and re-papering the walls. The kitchen had been whitewashed and looked fresh and clean. While Ethel unpacked the trunk I got to work on the kitchen range; the thing was choked up with odds and ends of

wallpaper, cigarette packets and painter's rags. Having cleared it, I took the bucket up the road to draw some water at Mrs Wilson's well and to buy firewood. Looking into the outhouse I was relieved to see some coal had arrived. Lighting the fire was easier than I had expected, and before long it was roaring away in fine style. 'Let's have some tea!' I shouted to Ethel – and then remembered there was no milk. This meant a journey down the lane to Edginton's farm. I came back with milk, butter and eggs. We had brought a loaf of bread and some jam with us.

While the kettle was boiling I went upstairs to see how the builders were getting on. The bedroom ceiling was finished and a man was washing the floor with a rag. Lifting a gloomy face to me, he said: 'You sleeping 'ere to-night?' I said that I was. He squeezed his rag into the bucket: 'I suppose you know the place is 'aunted?' he said. 'Really!' I answered. 'Yes, 'aunted,' he went on. 'That's what they say, and that's why the place wouldn't let.' I thanked him for

the information and went downstairs to pass on the startling news to
Ethel. She was no more disturbed about it than I. 'If the ghost
turns up,' she said, 'I shall get it to help me with the curtains.'

We had our tea sitting on the trunk, for as yet there was no
furniture. That was due to come the following morning from Dept-
ford, where it had been stored. We worked at cleaning up till nearly
nine, then had a scratch supper and camped out in blankets on the
sitting-room floor. No eldritch shrieks or rattling chains disturbed
our slumbers. As the furniture was not expected before midday, I
cycled to Cranleigh and bought a dinner service. It was of nonde-
script pattern and very cheap, but so strong that it lasted us for years.
I still have one of the plates – nothing will break it. Packed in a
small crate, the service was too heavy for my cycle and had to be
left for the carrier to deliver next day. Ethel and I had a bread-and-
cheese lunch and waited for the furniture. Then it began to rain.
The van arrived at three-thirty; of course the men had lost their way.
It was no fun carting the furniture indoors through the wet. The
men were in a hurry to get back to London and our things were
dumped anywhere. It was five o'clock when they left after drinking
gallons of tea.

Sorting out the furniture was troublesome; we had to get at the
beds and mattresses to sleep on that night. I made the kitchen
quite natty with the gate-legged table, the Dower Press and four
antique chairs. Mrs Chaplin's rugs looked well on the brick floor.
Ethel unpacked a bundle of assorted curtains and set to work on
them. There were no rods, but she cut them to fit the cottage windows and fixed them up temporarily. I spent the next afternoon
laying our carpet in the bedroom. The workmen had finished upstairs and were whitewashing the scullery and larder.

Before supper I took the bucket up the road to draw some water

and have a chat with Mrs Wilson. She was full of gossip and it was evident that she had never heard of our ghost. She had watched the arrival of our furniture with interest. 'They're moving in!' must have gone round the neighbourhood already, for the next morning I had a visit from an old man prepared to tackle the garden. After a look round he said: 'It ain't no good – no good at all. 'Tis all coochy.' However, he volunteered to come once a week. Soon after that the carrier arrived with my dinner service. He asked if there was anything I wanted in Guildford. I had yet to realize that the carrier was prepared to do one's shopping in the town – a practice much to be commended as he was the only means of public transport, this being before the advent of the country bus.

Cyril was due on Friday night; he had Saturday morning off. He arrived at nine o'clock, having cycled from Bramley. He was quite impressed by my cottage, which certainly looked its best at night. He brought with him a heavy and strangely shaped parcel which had been delivered at Hyde Vale by Shoolbred's van. We unpacked it and found a complete side of bacon, a present from Aunt Fanny. We hung it up in our small larder and it provided delicious rashers for months.

With Cyril's help we got things straight. Together we laid in the sitting-room the carpet from our old home which had always been a favourite of mine – it was a darkish green with a border of flowers. On Sunday I borrowed a fag-hook from Mr Wilson and Cyril got to

work on the jungle in the garden while I tried to get the weeds out of the brick path in front of the cottage; Ethel cooked our meal with eggs and some bacon cut from Aunt Fanny's gift.

After supper we talked over their plans for the future. Cyril was now with a firm of Underwriters at Lloyd's and was earning a good salary. As Ethel was teaching at the Blackheath Conservatoire of Music and wished to remain in the district, the pair of them planned to rent a house in Lee or Blackheath after I was married. Next morning Cyril had to catch an early train to London. Ethel and I stayed on for a couple of days to see the work finished. Then after a last look round, I left the key with Mrs Wilson and we returned to town.

I went to Norbury the following day and told Pie of our experiences at the cottage. When I came to the ghost she was highly interested and wanted to know all about it. I explained that it could not have been a very obtrusive ghost or Mrs Wilson would have heard of it. Certainly it never had any substance as far as we were concerned, for though we lived in the cottage for six years we never saw it, nor did any of our friends. While I was away Pie had received a cheque from her godmother. Our cash presents now amounted to £45; and we also had a little money saved, so we felt quite rich. With the addition of our united earnings from painting, we could face the future with confidence.

The arrangements for the wedding were now virtually complete; even Pie's wedding dress was nearly finished. I cannot describe it though I heard reports on it from her sisters, but I do know that she looked lovely on the day. When that day came Ethel, Cyril and I were up early. Cyril, as my Best Man, put the ring carefully in his waistcoat pocket. We both wore frock-coats – though how I acquired mine I cannot now imagine. I was terribly nervous and so anxious to be in time that we reached the church much too early. Thereafter all went well. Pie's uncle, the wine importer, gave her away, and afterwards, at the reception, gave me a bottle of a rather special wine to drink at our first meal in our cottage. Aunt Fanny was in great form and was introduced to all her new relations; she and Mrs Chaplin got on famously. We had a terrific send-off from a bodyguard of our fellow students as we drove away to the station.

The train from London set us down at Chilworth. I had ordered a fly to meet us and it was waiting at the station. The evening was misty, quite thick on the common by Wonersh, and the driver lost his way, but I was able to redirect him and, as we turned the corner by Mrs Wilson's, Pie leant from the carriage window to catch her first sight of our cottage.

Lights already shone from the windows and the front door stood open. When we stopped I got out. 'Come on,' I said, 'I'm going to carry you over the threshold.' 'You are certainly not. You are much too tired. You'd probably drop me – and the wine as well.' So I gave in. Annie Gregory was waiting in the doorway to greet us, and a lovely smell of dinner came from the kitchen. 'I never thought

I should get ready in time,' she said, 'so I'm thankful you're late. Having no water laid on, and having to find everything! . . . However, it's all ready now.'

I took Pie upstairs, carrying a candle, to show her the rooms. A cheerful fire was burning in our bedroom, and there were flowers on our chest of drawers. We looked into the spare room and the little room under the eaves. Pie said: 'I think it's quite sweet. You know, it's not as small as I expected. And I love the kitchen.'

Downstairs I unpacked our bottle of wine – fortunately I had remembered a corkscrew. We had no wineglasses but I poured the wine into tumblers. Annie had laid the dinner on our gate-legged table and it looked very inviting with our four brass candlesticks, the red checked cloth and a bowl of Michaelmas daisies. We asked her to stop and share our meal. 'I can't keep the fly waiting,' she explained (it was to take her back to Bramley). 'Besides, there is the train to catch.' Then she turned to Pie: 'You and Ernest must come over to Milford soon and while Ernest talks art with Carl I can give you some tips on cooking.' Taking my hand she said: 'Carl and the girls send you their love and good wishes. Now I must be off.' We all drank to happy days and I took a glass out to the driver. We waved goodbye from our front door as they drove away.

It was quite dark by this time and the mist made it cold outside. The only sound was a pheasant squawking in the copse opposite. We turned and went into the kitchen and sat down to the first meal in our own home. We were too tired to think of washing up afterwards; I just put the things in the sink and pumped water on them. Before we went to bed we looked out the special treasures we had brought with us – the panel portrait of my grandmother by Thomas Dicksee; the charming little nude by Chaplin, the Belgian artist; Pie's enamel patch box and her tiny china mouse.

We were very happy. Pie's mural at Guy's Hospital had been triumphantly finished. I had a picture accepted by the Royal Academy, hung on the line and sold for £100. We were married, and between us we had savings and wedding presents in cash amounting to perhaps £70. What had seemed impossible a few months earlier had come to pass, and we thanked God for our cottage home.

Also by E. H. Shepard
available from Methuen

DRAWN FROM MEMORY

'An enchanted book, warm with muffin fires and bright
with untrammelled innocence'
Daily Mail

In this delightful autobiography E. H. Shepard describes a classic
Victorian childhood. Shepard grew up in St John's Wood in the
1880s, with his brother Cyril and sister Ethel, among domestic
servants and maiden aunts, in an age when horse-drawn buses
and hansom cabs crowded the streets. *Drawn from Memory*
recalls this time with great charm and humour, and Shepard
illustrates the scenes of his young life with more than 120 of his
inimitable drawings.

'*Drawn from Memory* recreates a vanished age with unusual
clarity . . . text and pictures combine with the happiest effect'
Times Literary Supplement

'This is one of those books that have all the marks of a classic'
Country Life

SELECTED BIOGRAPHY AND AUTOBIOGRAPHY TITLES
AVAILABLE FROM METHUEN

	ISBN	TITLE	AUTHOR	PRICE
☐	0 413 73120 0	Alan Ayckbourn: Grinning at the Edge	Paul Allen	£19.99
☐	0 413 70600 1	David Garrick	Jean Benedetti	£20.00
☐	0 413 77129 6	Gielgud: a theatrical life	Jonathan Croall	£8.99
☐	0 413 74060 9	Drink to the Bird	Benedict Kiely	£6.99
☐	0 413 75120 1	The Waves Behind Us	Benedict Kiely	£7.99
☐	0 413 77168 7	Home Before Night	Hugh Leonard	£7.99
☐	0 413 77148 2	Out After Dark	Hugh Leonard	£7.99
☐	0 413 77340 X	Timebends	Arthur Miller	£9.99
☐	0 413 73050 6	Double Act: a life of Tom Stoppard	Ira Nadel	£25.00
☐	0 413 75300 X	Drawn from Memory	E. H. Shepard	£9.99
☐	0 413 75190 2	Aké: memoirs of a Nigerian childhood	Wole Soyinka	£7.99
☐	0 413 75200 3	Isará	Wole Soyinka	£7.99
☐	0 413 74420 5	Ibadan	Wole Soyinka	£7.99
☐	0 413 76710 8	Shakespeare: the poet and his plays	Stanley Wells	£10.99

★ All Methuen travel titles are available through mail order or from your local bookshop, or online at www.methuen.co.uk

Please send cheque/eurocheque/postal order (sterling only) Access, Visa, Mastercard, Diners Card, Switch or Amex.

Expiry Date: .... Signature: ....

Please allow 75 pence per book for post and packing U.K.

Overseas customers please allow £1.00 per copy for post and packing.

ALL ORDERS TO:

Methuen Books, Books by Post, TBS Limited, The Book Service, Colchester Road, Frating Green, Colchester, Essex CO7 7DW.

NAME:...

ADDRESS:

....

....

....

Please allow 28 days for delivery. Please tick box if you do not wish to receive any additional information ☐

Prices and availability subject to change without notice.